Drawing

FIGURES

By

Ajay

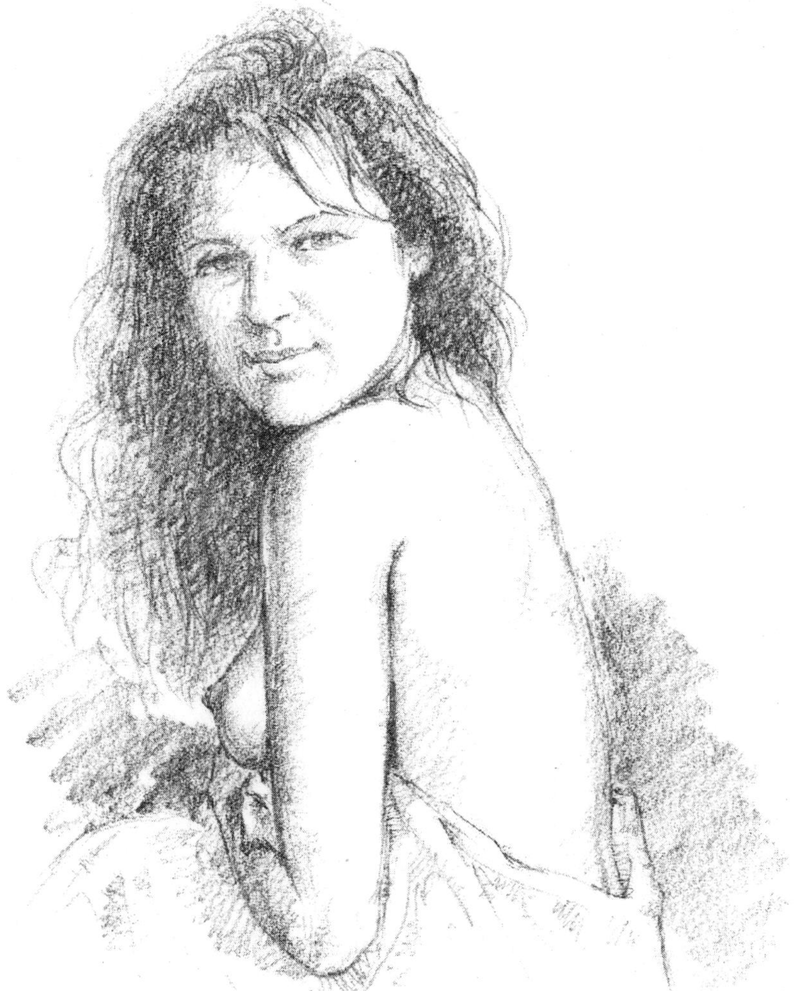

UNICORN BOOKS

ISBN: 978-81-7806-161-0

UNICORN BOOKS Pvt. Ltd, J-3/16, Darya Ganj, New Delhi-110002
Phones: 23276539, 23272783/84, Fax: 23257790
E-mail: unicornbooks@vsnl.com
Website: www.unicornbooks.in

Contents

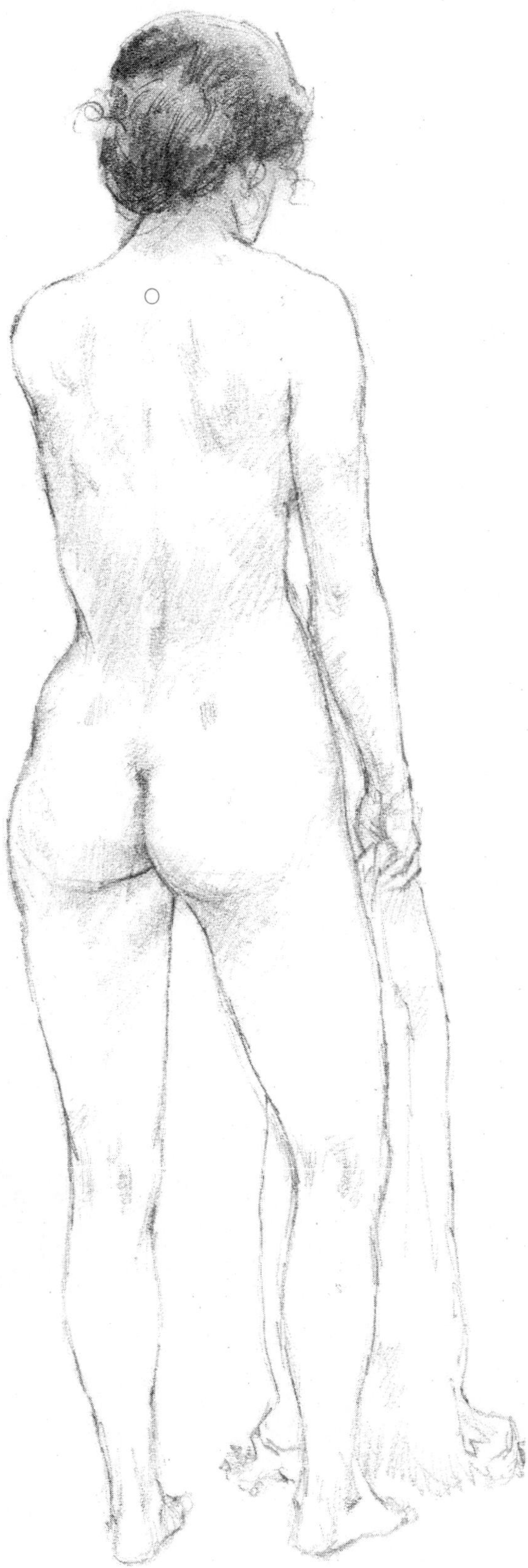

Introduction

While we would need a hundred words to speak about something, a drawing can express the same thing very beautifully without the help of a single word. So, in this book I would like to speak to you through my sketches.

This book neither deals with the difficulties which are involved in drawing, nor is it an attempt to turn you into an expert of human anatomy. It is rather about drawing instinctively.

Draw in an easy manner. With the passage of time, you would become perfect in handling your pencil and in using paper and its various textures. I have used white cartridge paper, tinted paper and mount board as the working surfaces for these drawings. For good results and satisfaction, you can use 2B, 4B, 6B and black conte crayon pencils. You can use any of these pencils according to your choice.

Take a long look at the subject and check the proportion and the negative space and then simply start drawing it on a paper. Your eyes should focus on the three dimensional form of an object. It is not an outline, but a thing which contains volume. So, try and draw around it. The tones should never stop at the outline but move in and around the subject and describe its forms.

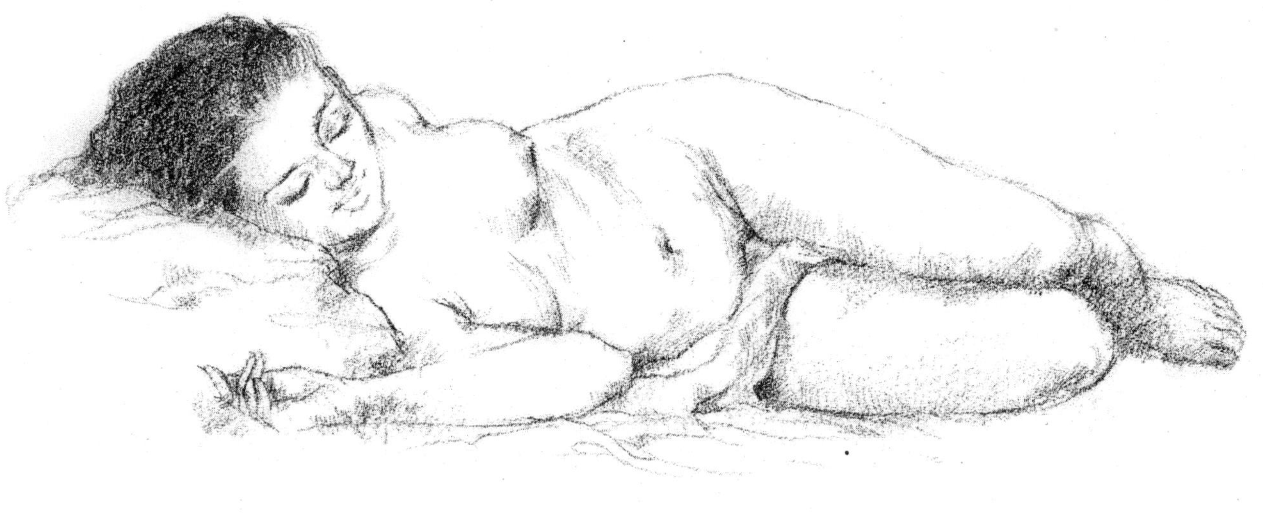

Anatomy

To draw something correctly, the basic structure of the anatomy of a figure should always be there at the back of your mind. It is nice and useful to get some knowledge about the basic proportion and anatomy of the human figure.

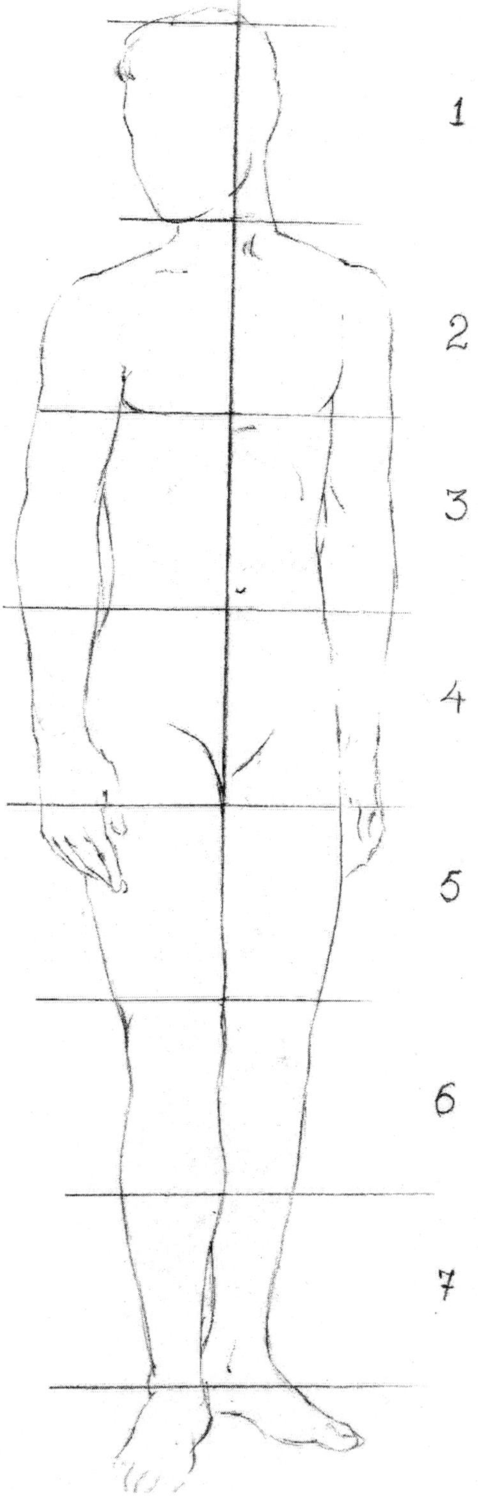

In an average human figure, the length of the body is seven and half times more than the body. The width of the shoulders is twice the size of the head, the waist size is equal to the size of one head and the hips are about one and half times the size of the head. You can divide a standing figure in three equal parts, first, from the chin to the pelvic bone, second, from the pelvic bone to the knee cap and the third, from the knee cap to the heel.

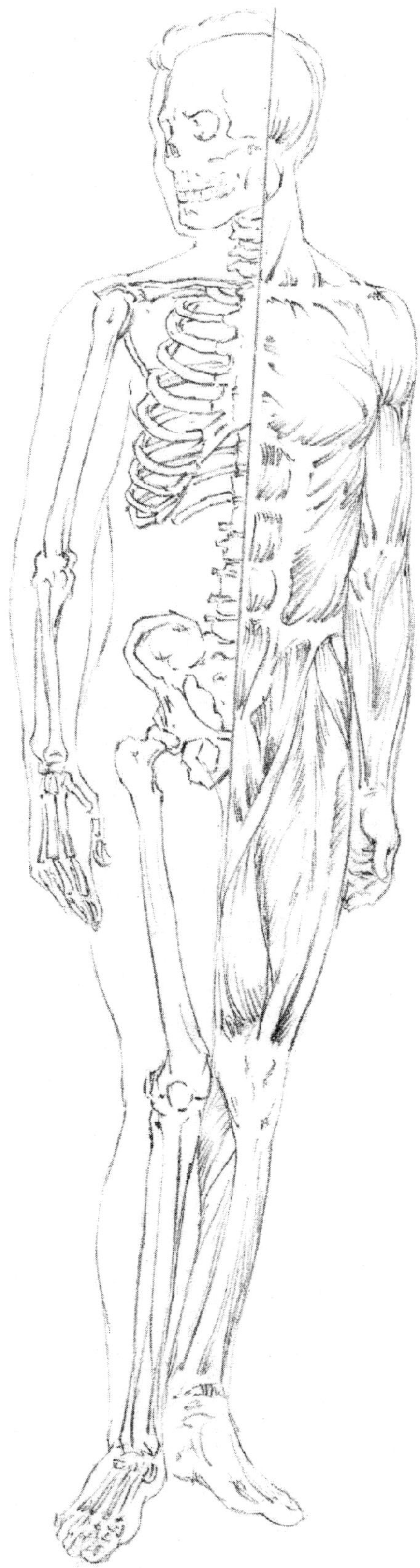

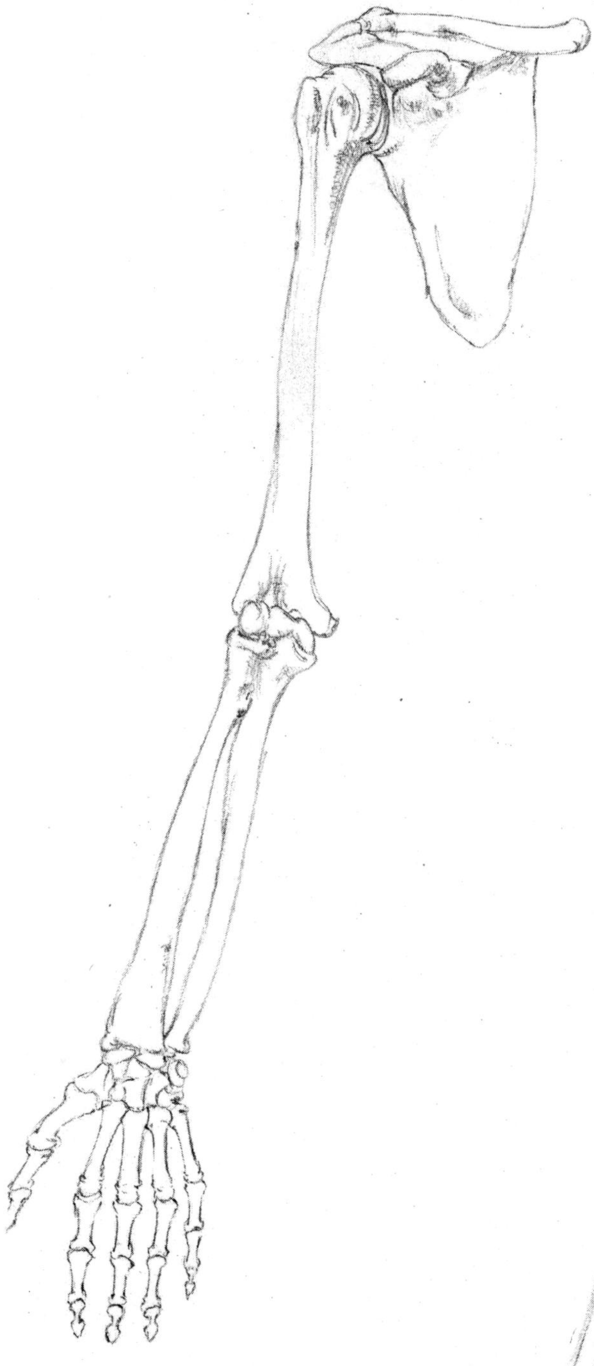

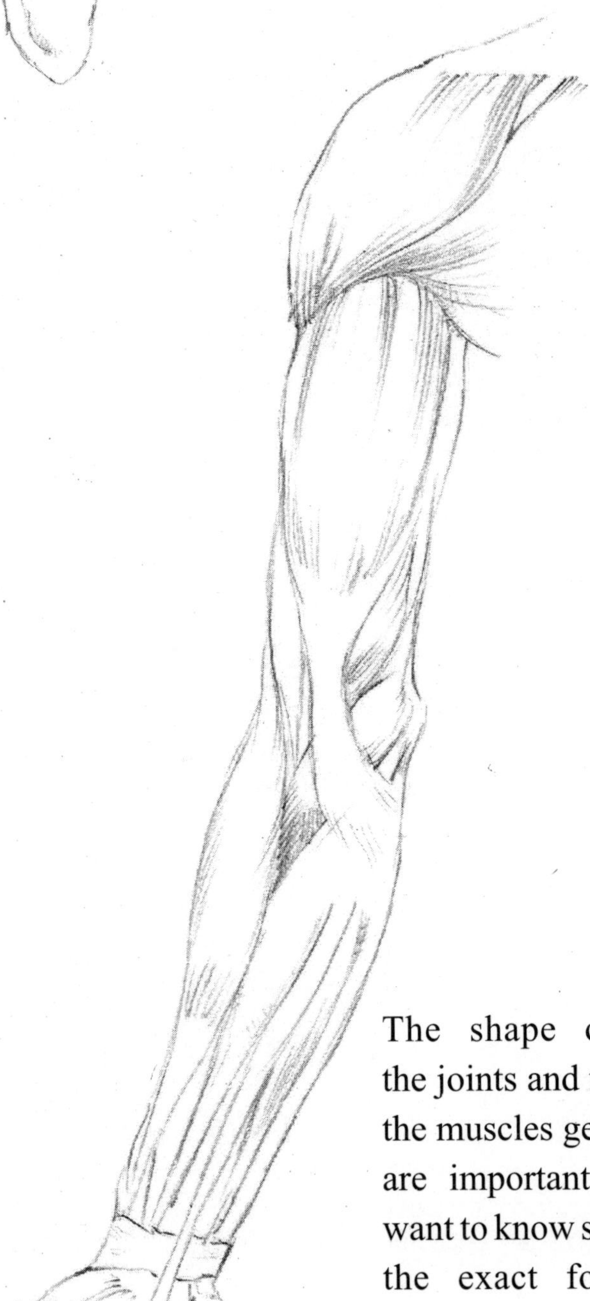

The shape of the bones, the joints and the place where the muscles get connected, all are important factors if we want to know something about the exact formation of a human body.

It is always helpful to know something about the bones, muscles and the tissues of the human body. You don't have to remember the latin names but the size, formation and the weight of its various parts.

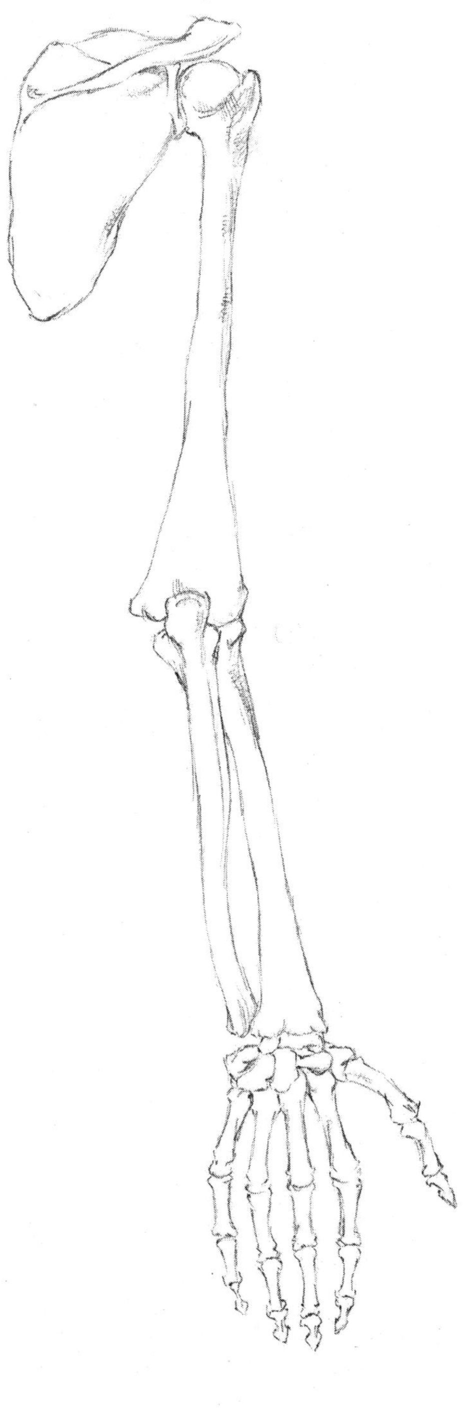

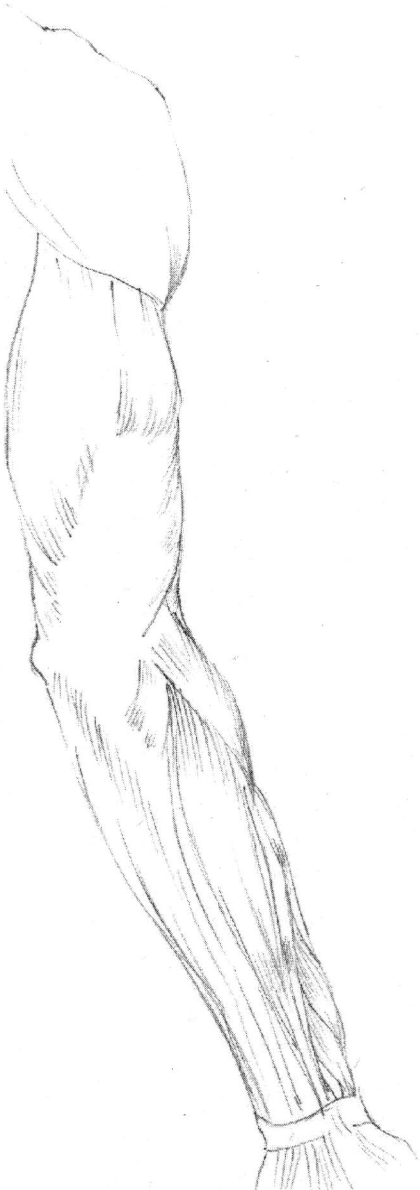

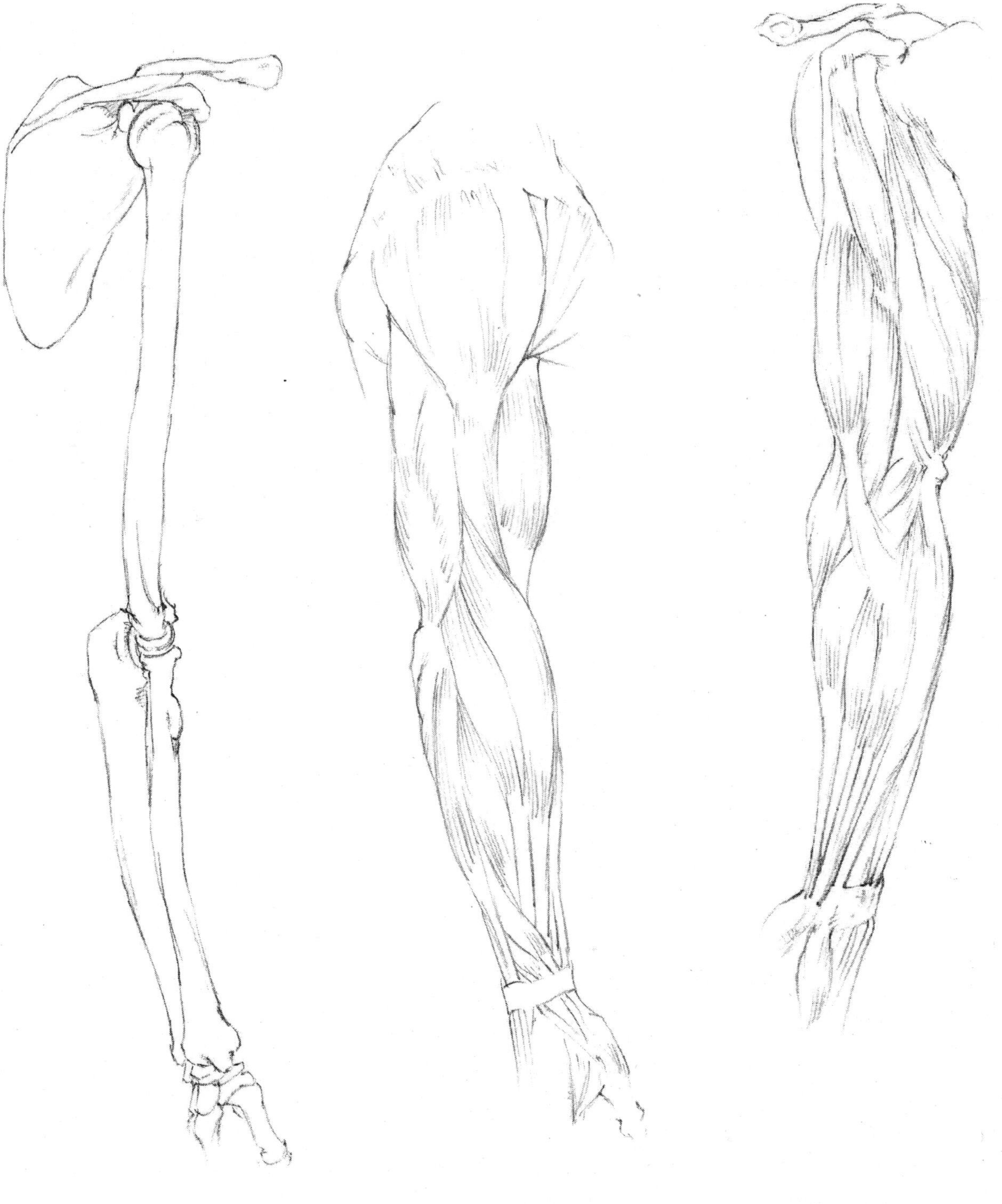

Texture and the curvatures of a certain part change with the posture and you should be able to capture that difference. Intelligent observation of a drawing or sketch will teach you a lot more than a good book on anatomy.

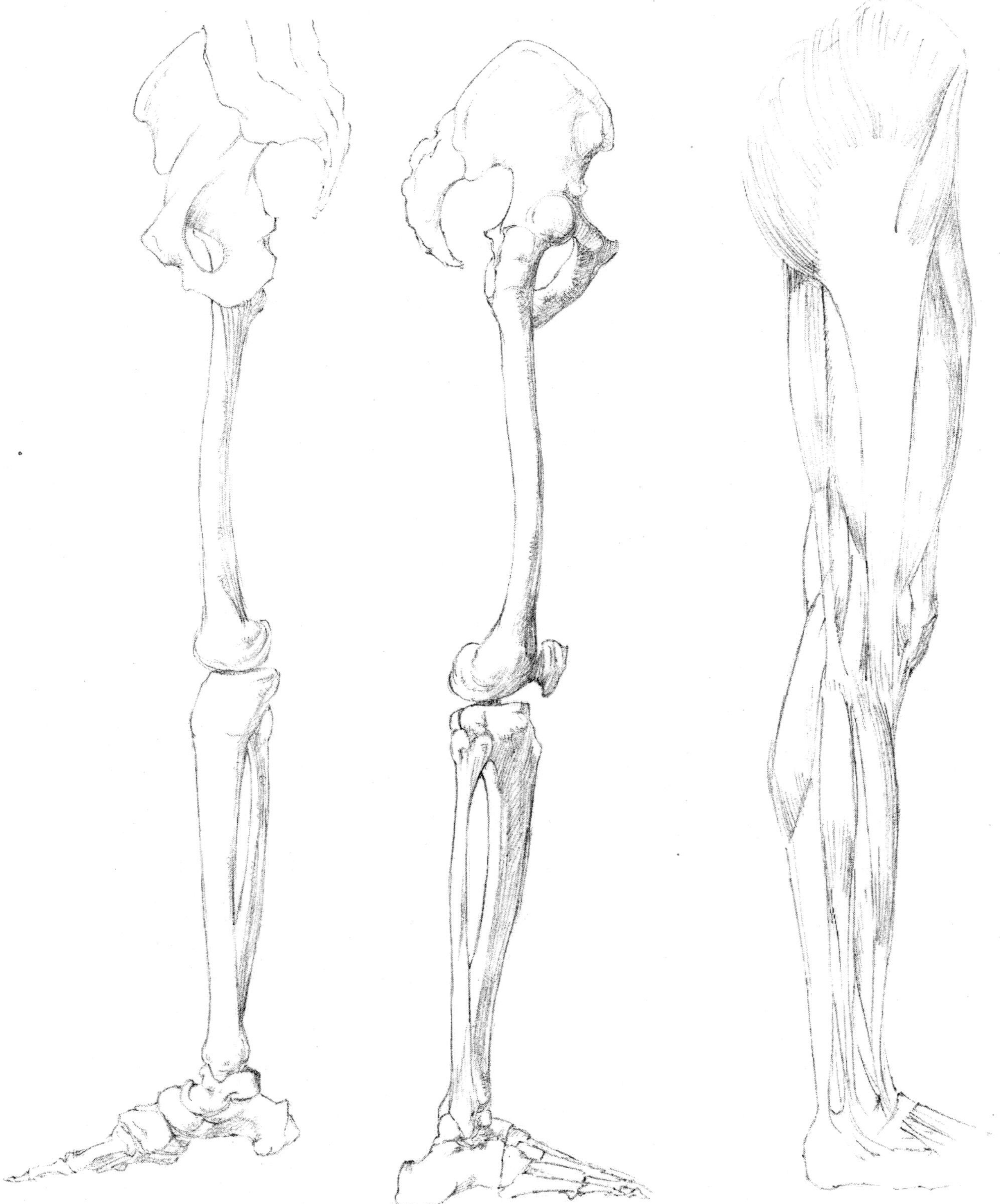

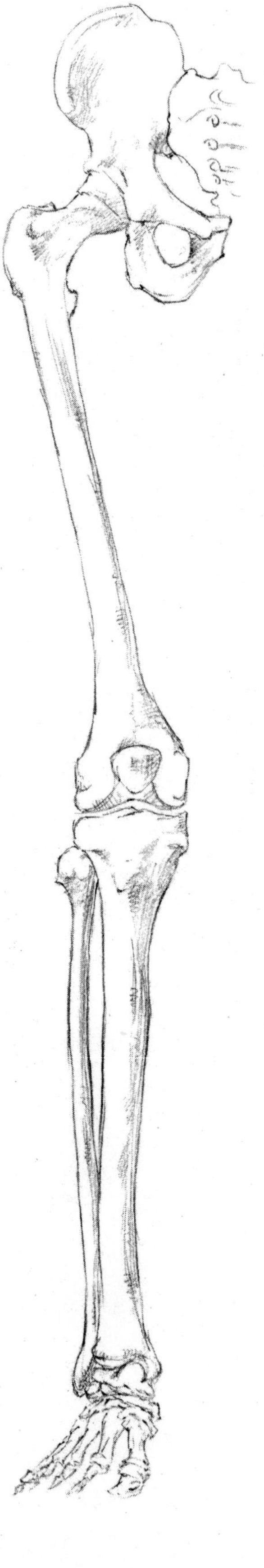

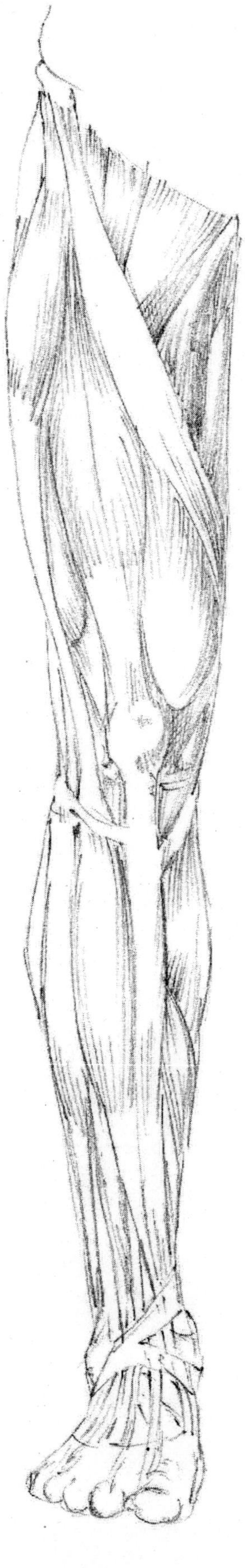

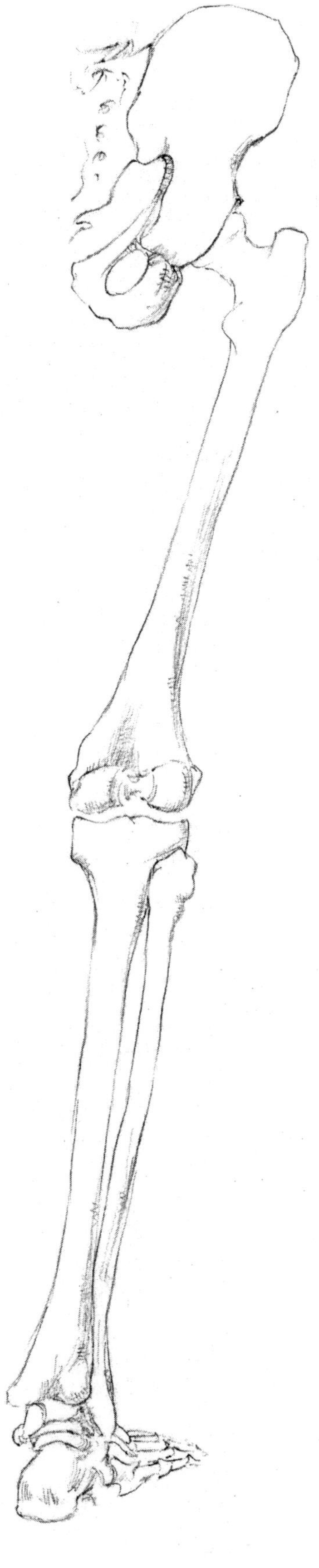

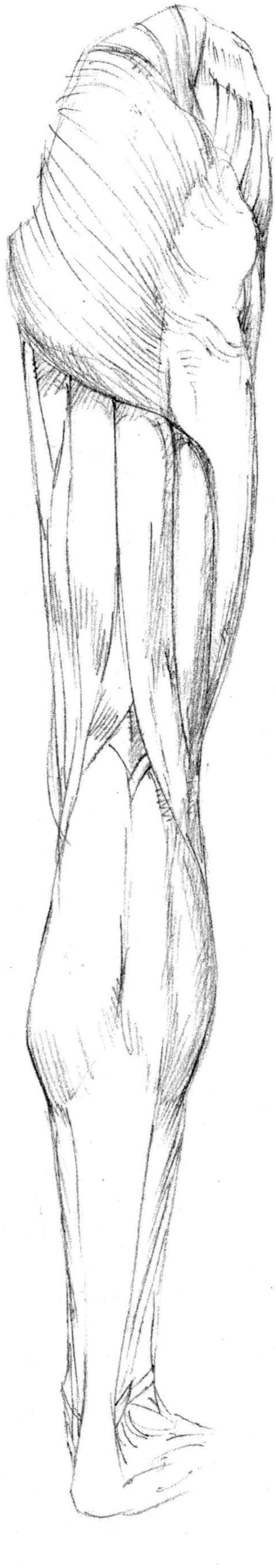

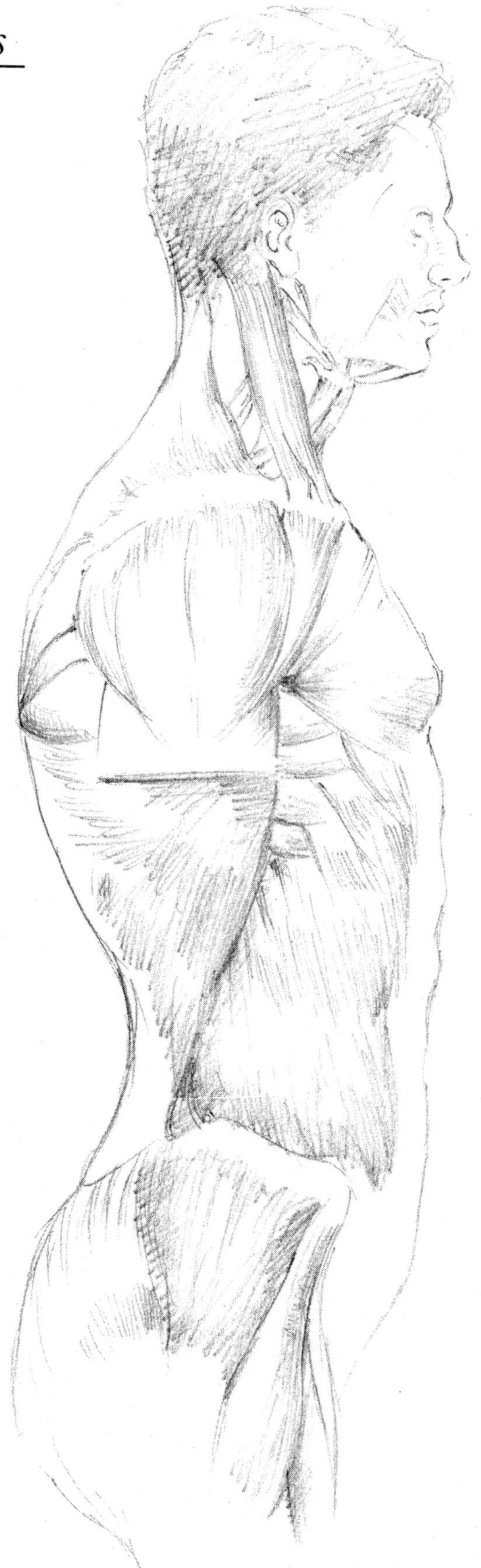

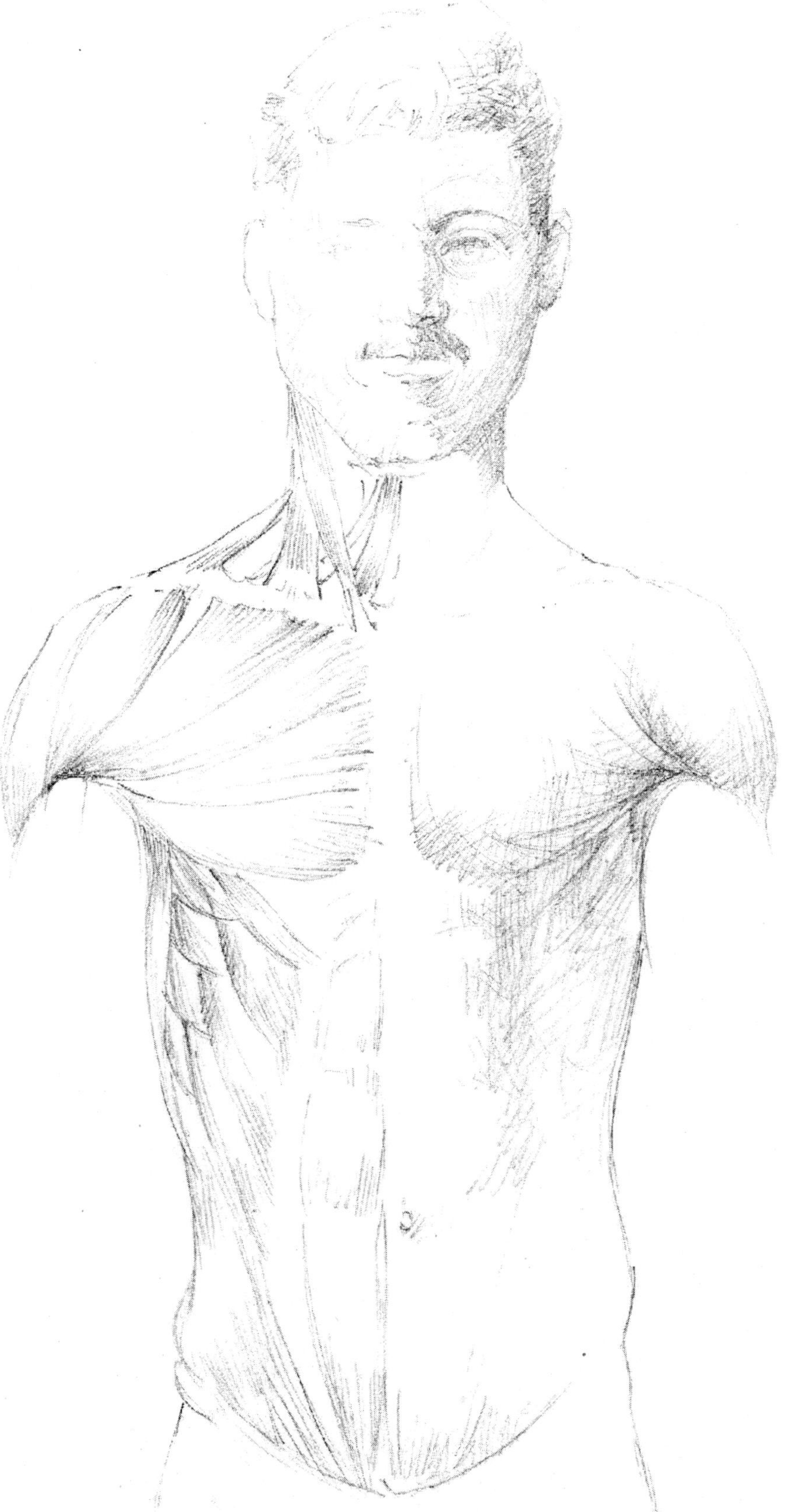

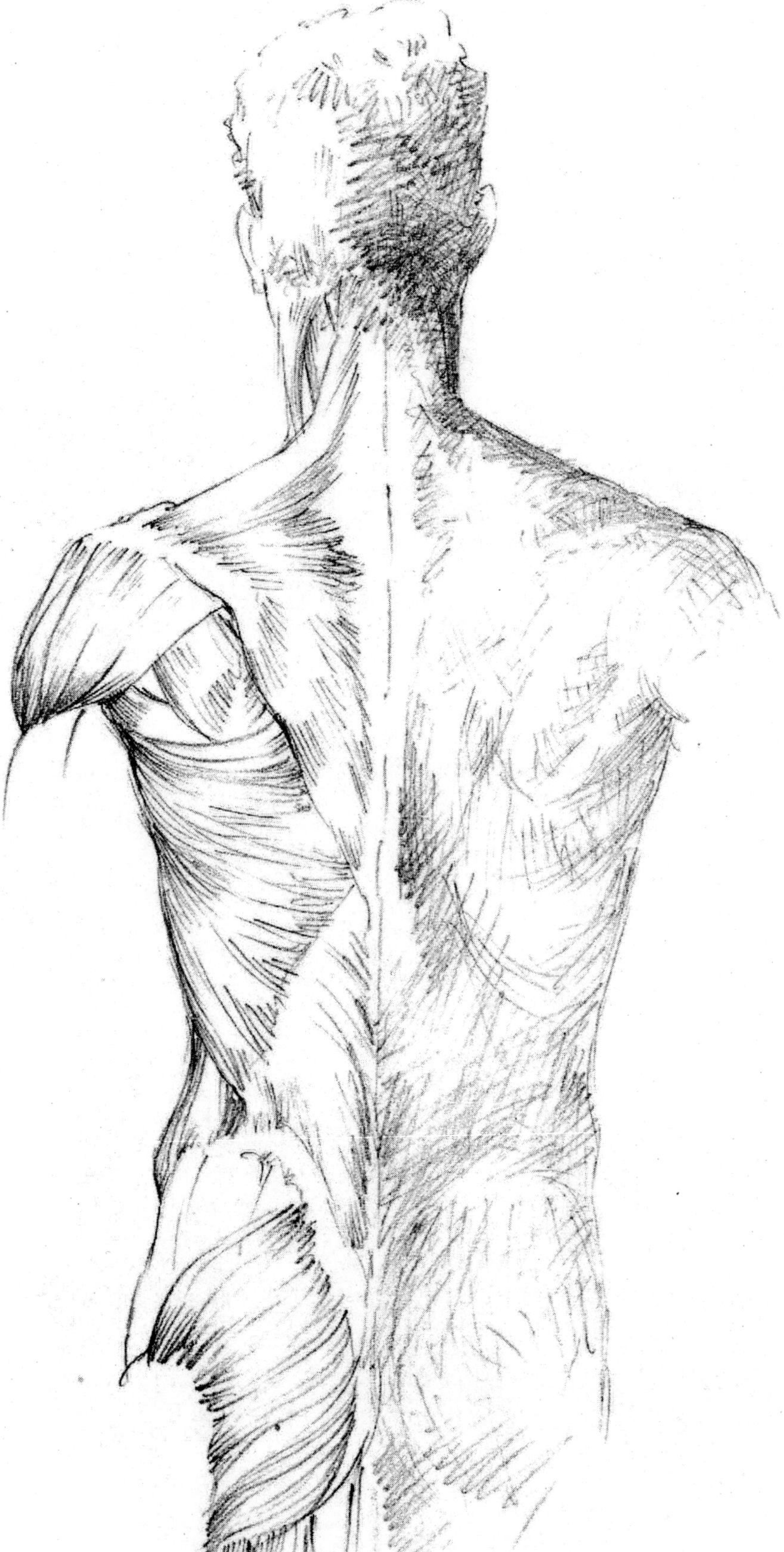

Lines & Strokes

Mark the centre line and the main joints which are going to affect the posture of your subject. Now draw the volume carefully and then add the shades wherever required.

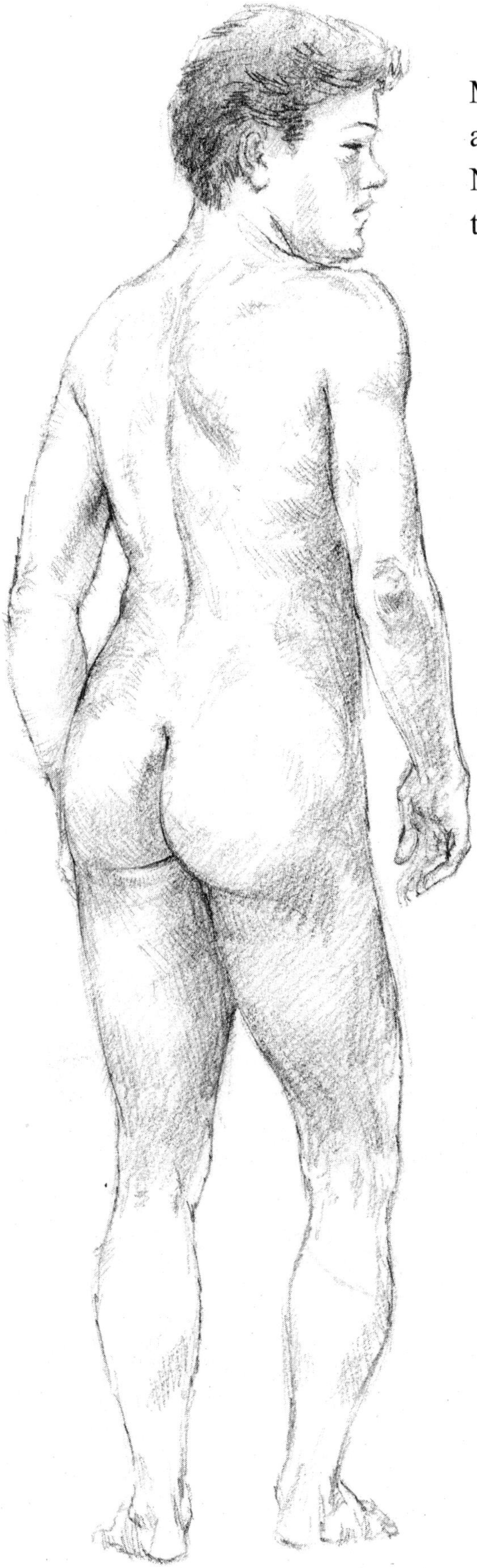

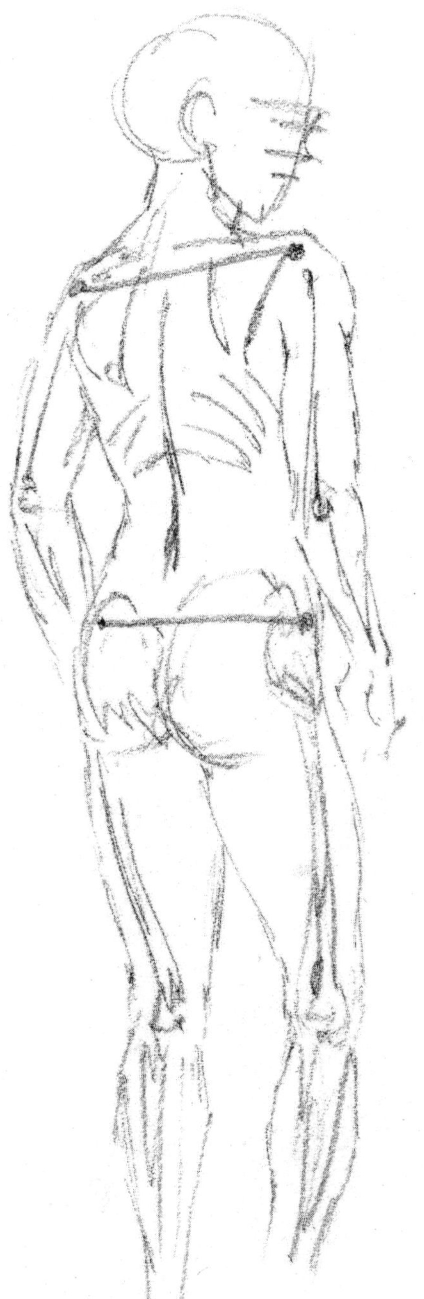

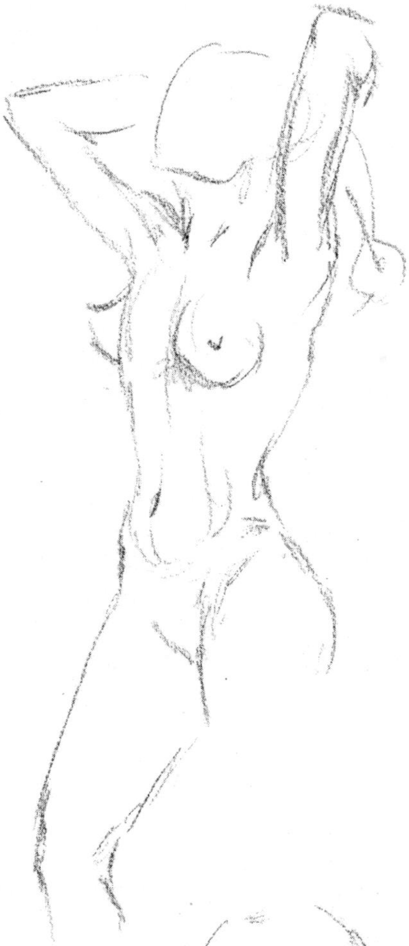

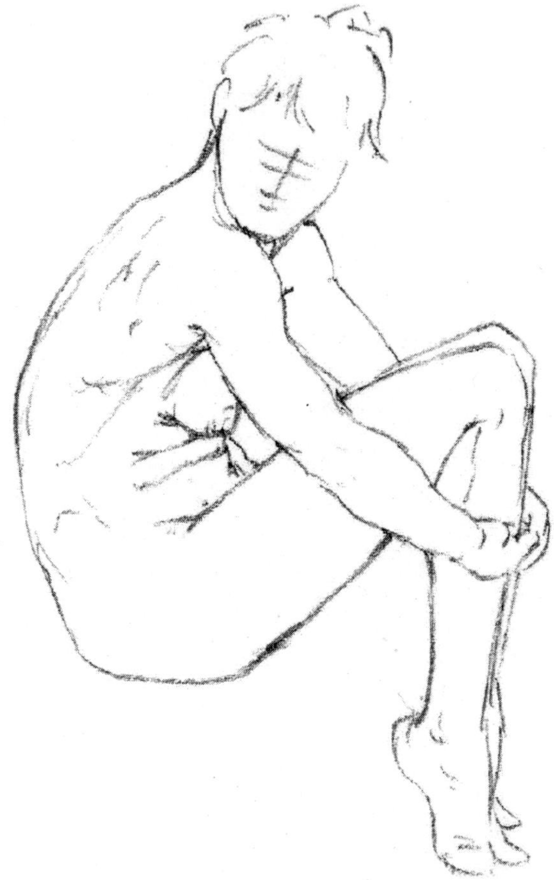

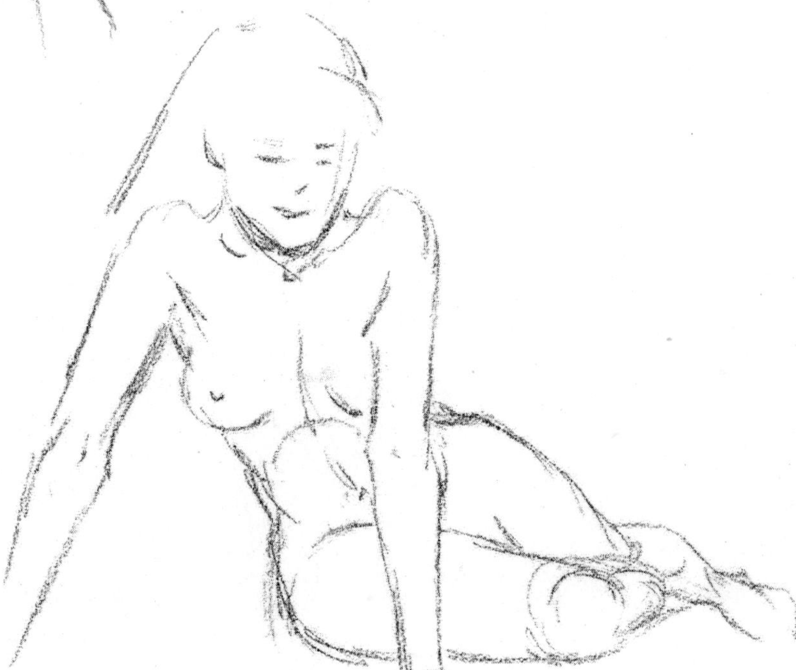

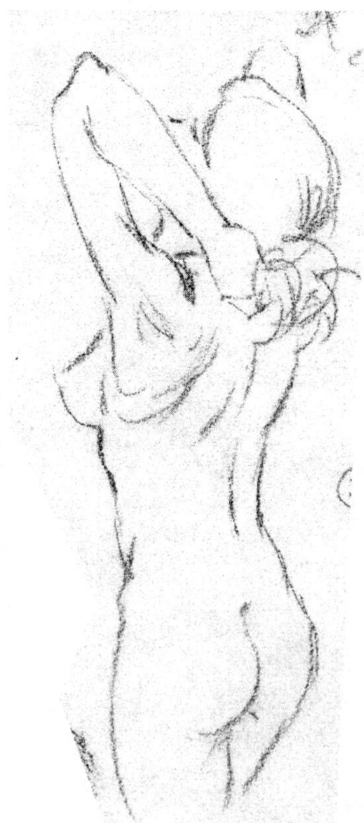

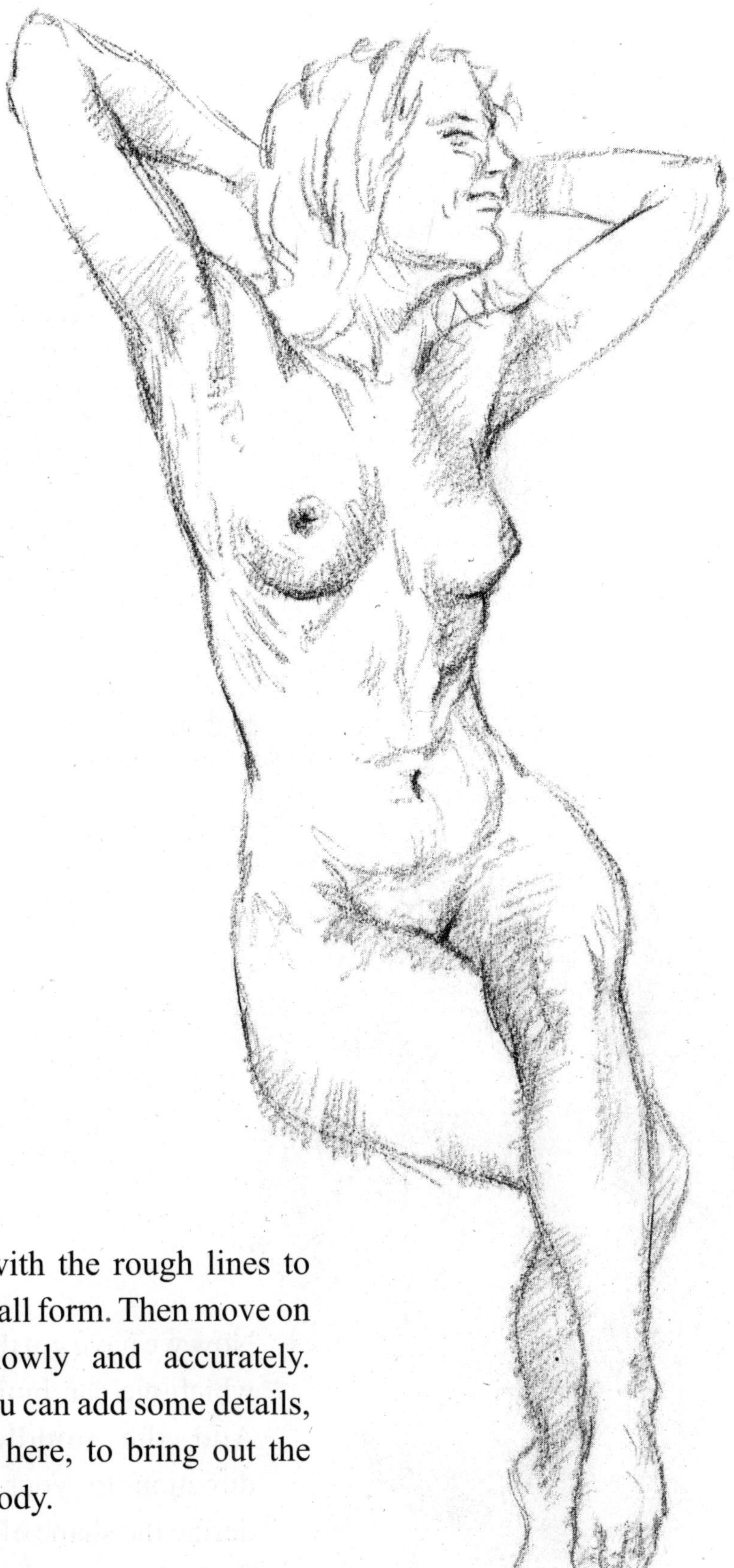

Start drawing with the rough lines to capture the overall form. Then move on to define it slowly and accurately. At this stage, you can add some details, as I have done here, to bring out the volume of the body.

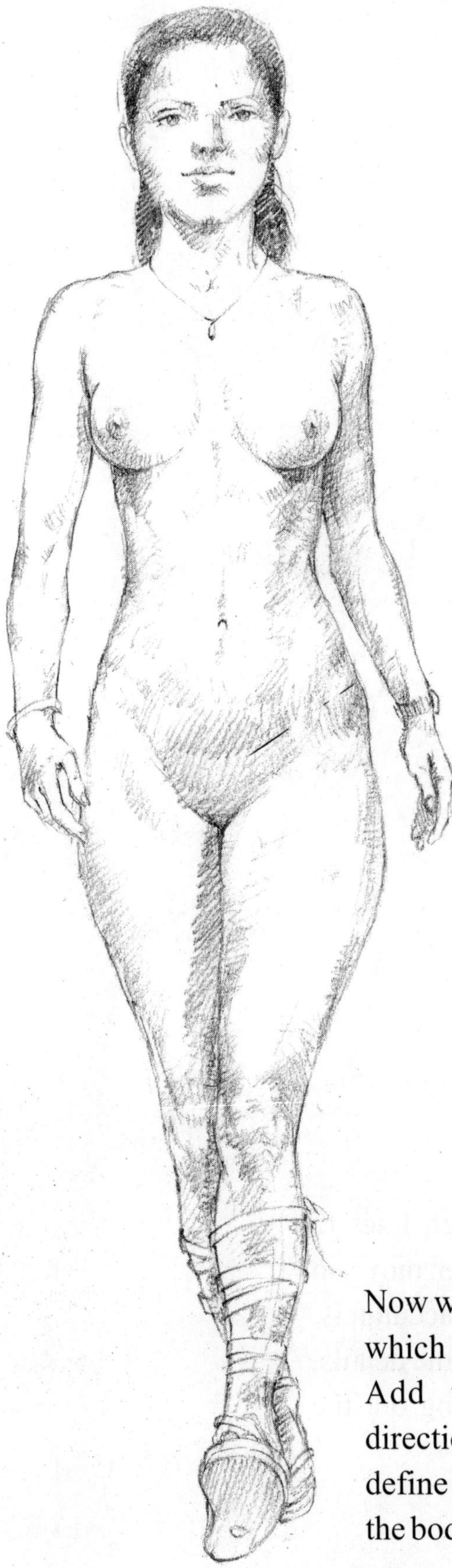

Now we have got the foundation on which we can build our structure. Add the middle tones, give direction to your stroke. It will define the shape of a certain part of the body.

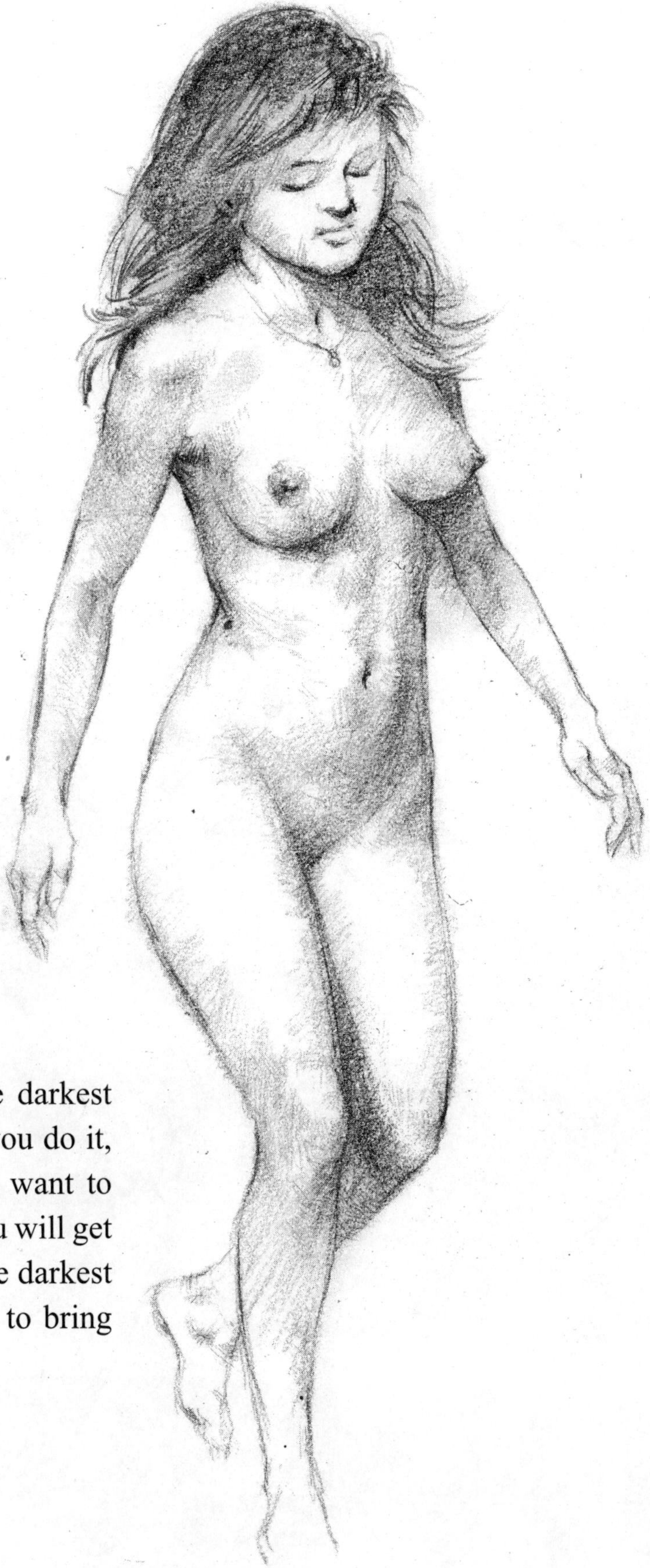

This is the time to create the darkest shades and shadows. Before you do it, rub in those parts which you want to diffuse by the fingertip and you will get an excellent light tone. Use the darkest pencil and sufficient pressure to bring out the jet black tone.

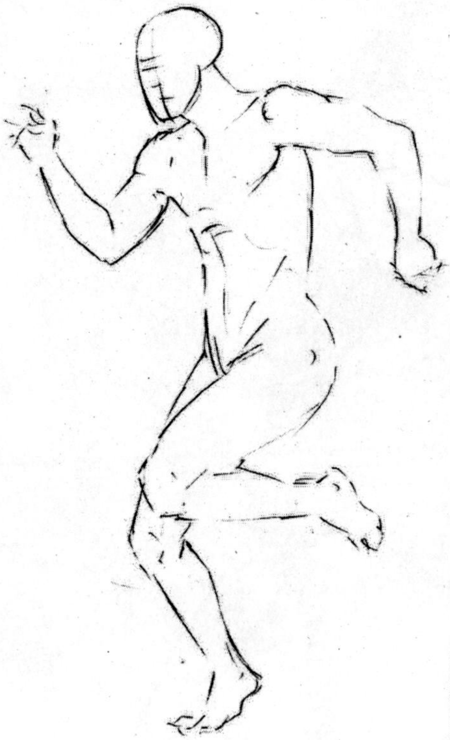

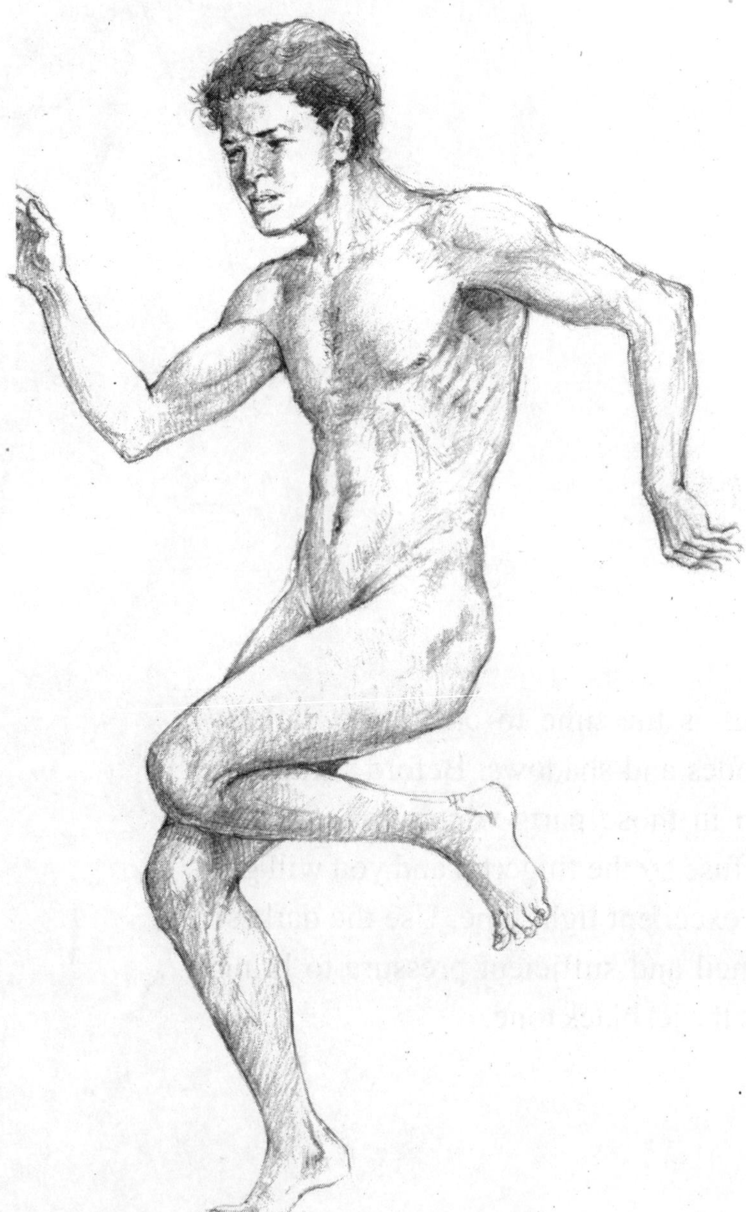

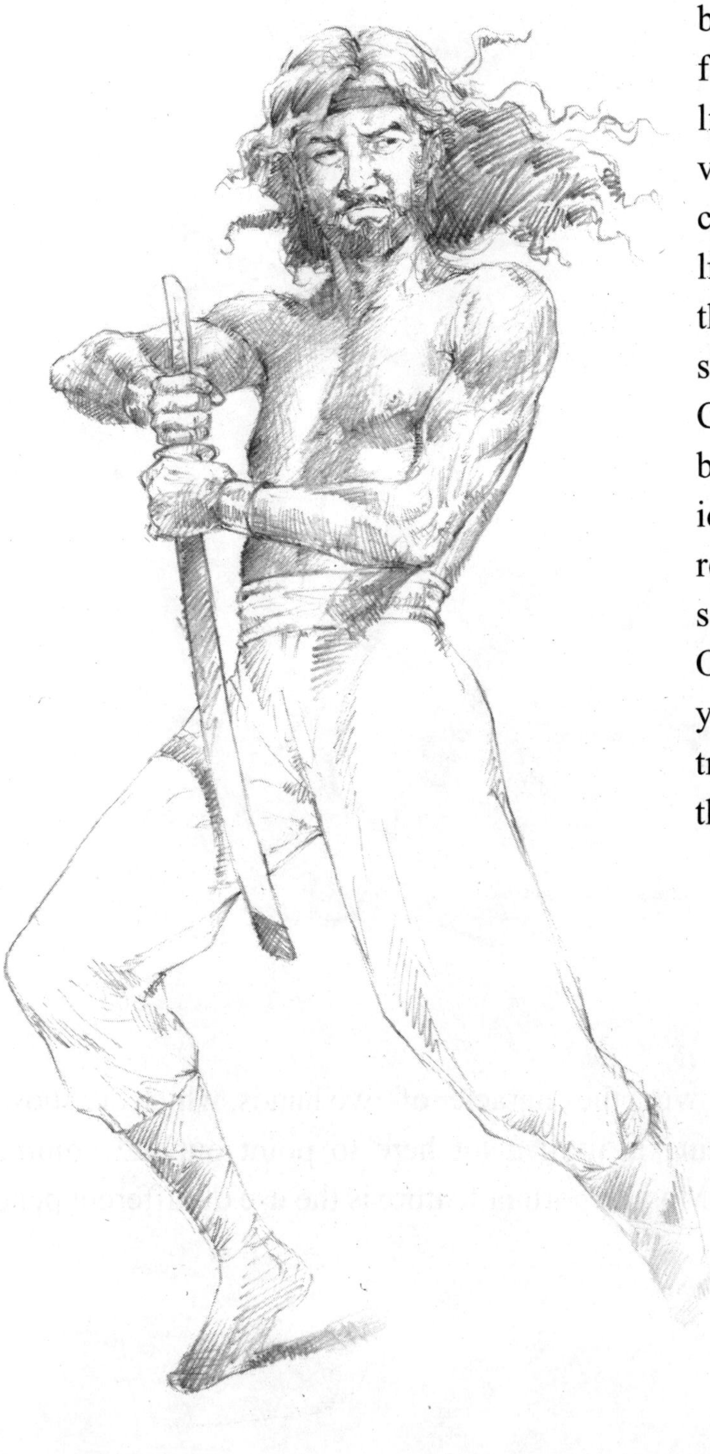

Study the basic form as much as you can because it is the foundation on which light plays and produces volume. Observe carefully the angle of light on certain parts of the body and study the shade it has created. Compare it with the basic forms and try to identify the one which is related to this particular section of the body. Once you have done it, you will never have trouble again in drawing this area of the body.

How to Draw Hands

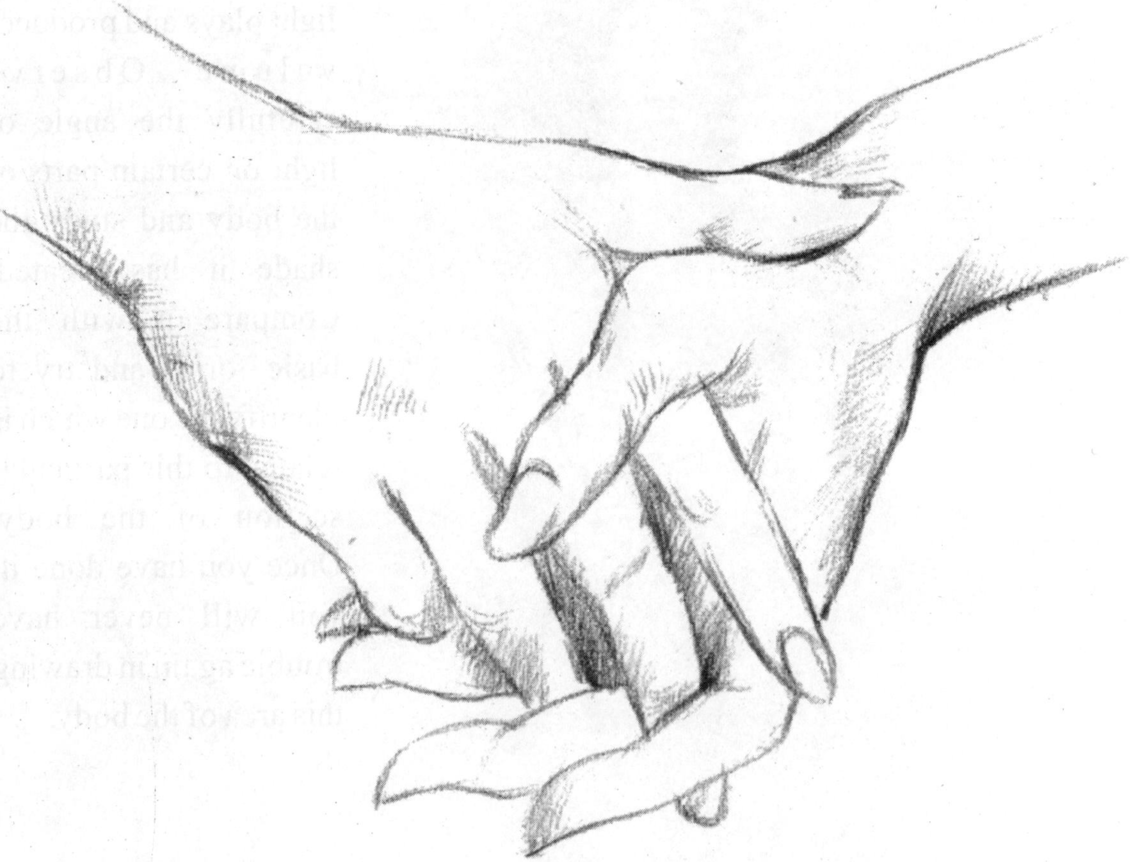

In this picture, we are showing the character of two hands, which are shown holding each other. Pencil shading is used a lot here to point out the volume and the movement of the hands. Most important feature is the use of different pencil strokes at different places.

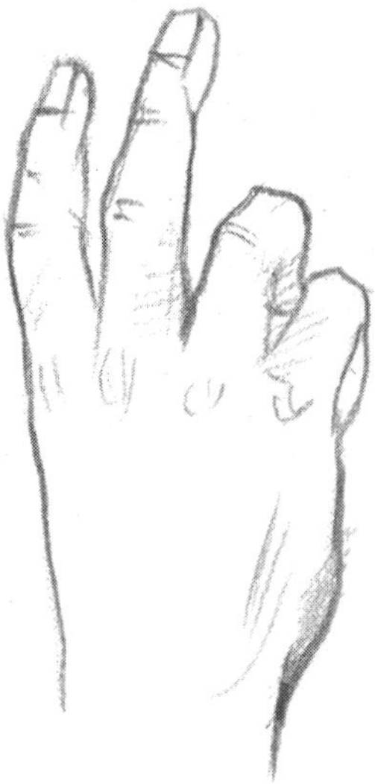

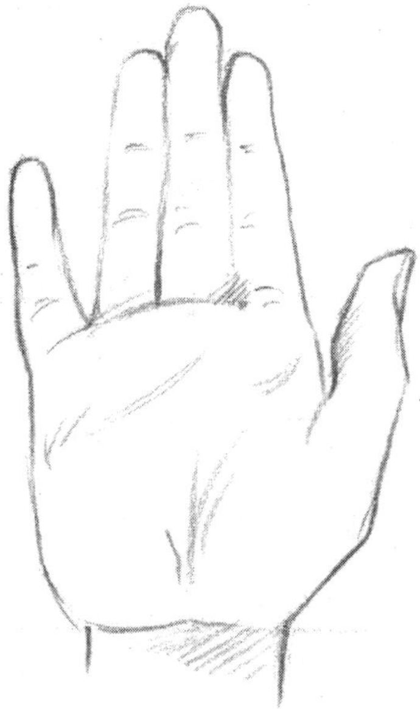

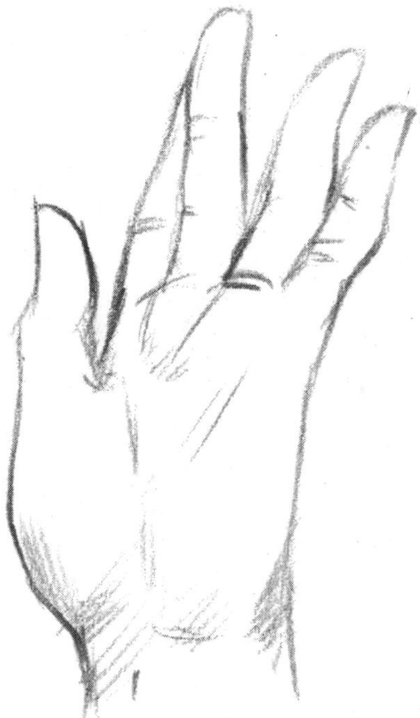

We start by drawing a hand. Then we move on to drawing two hands. We can draw these pictures step by step with the help of blocks. Care should be taken while doing line drawing, because it is difficult to draw the palm of a hand. So, we should pay attention at every line stroke.

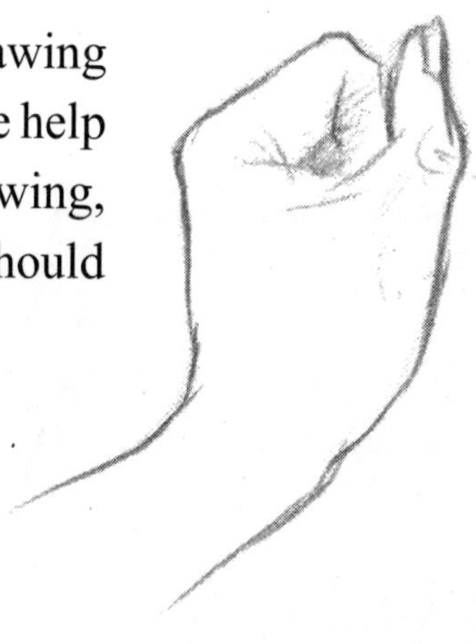

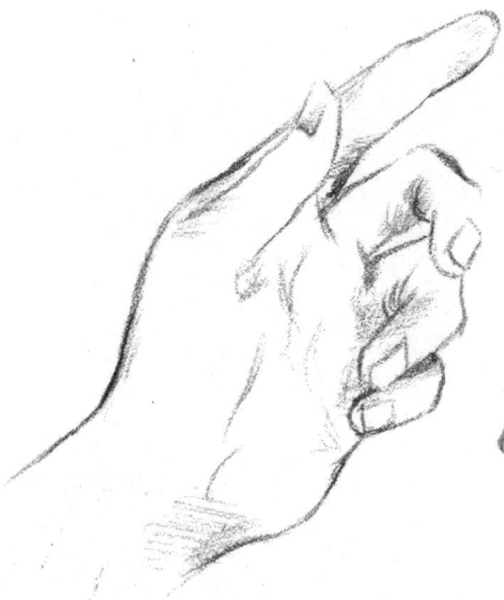

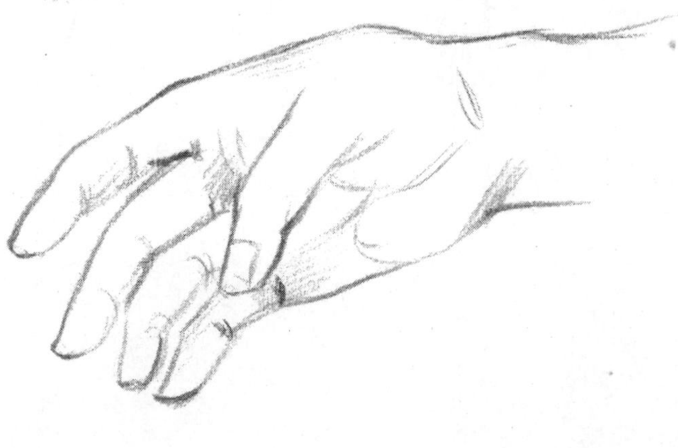

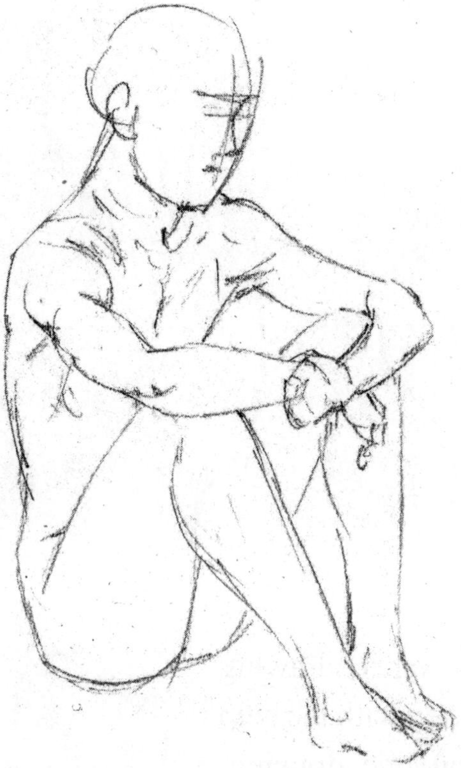

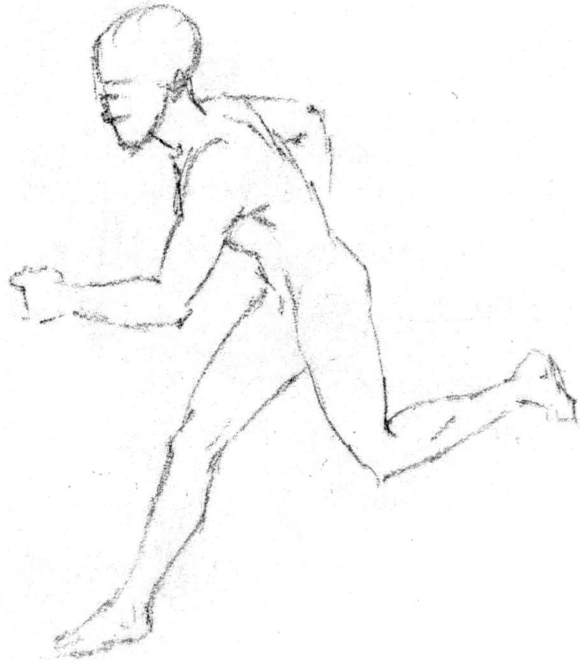

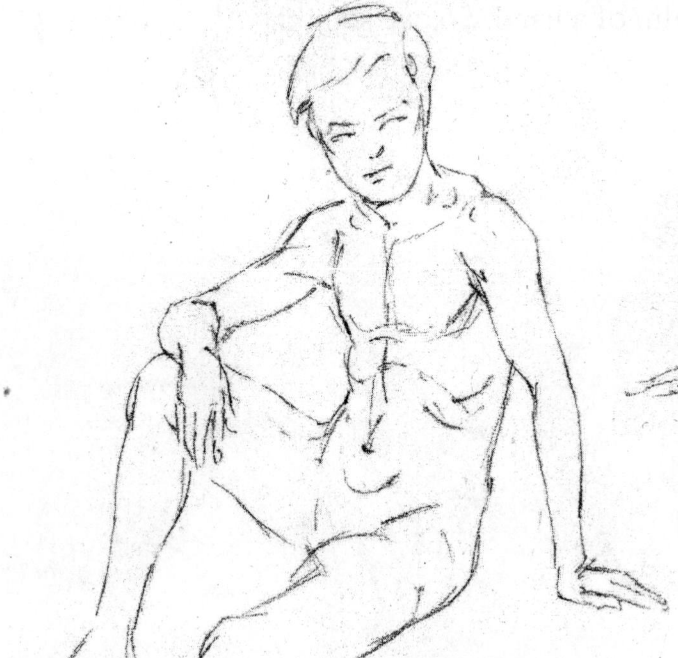

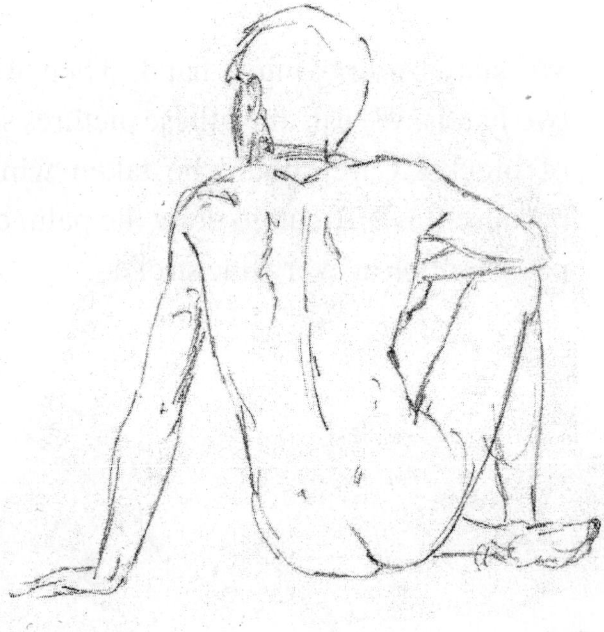

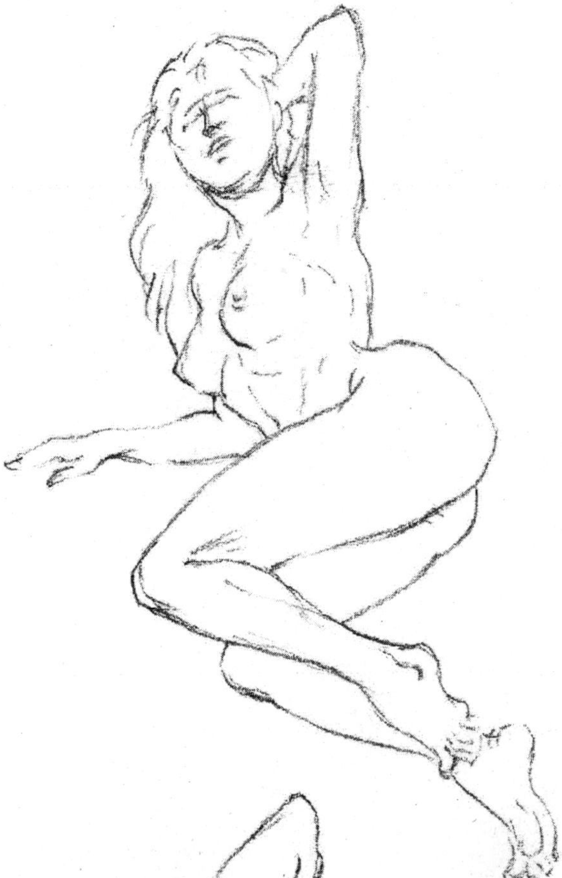

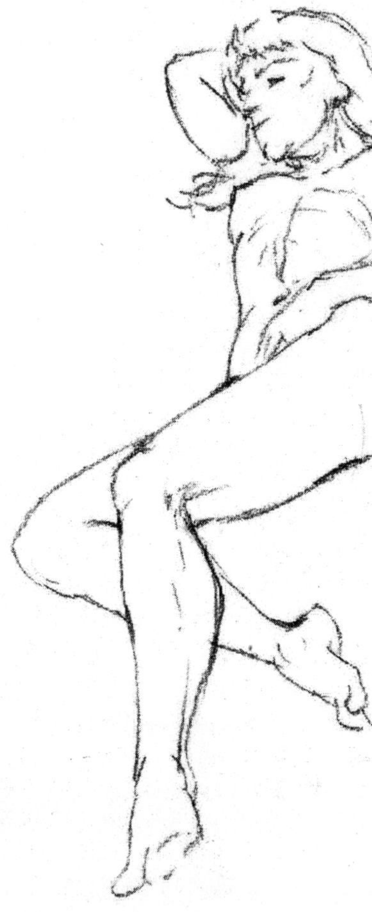

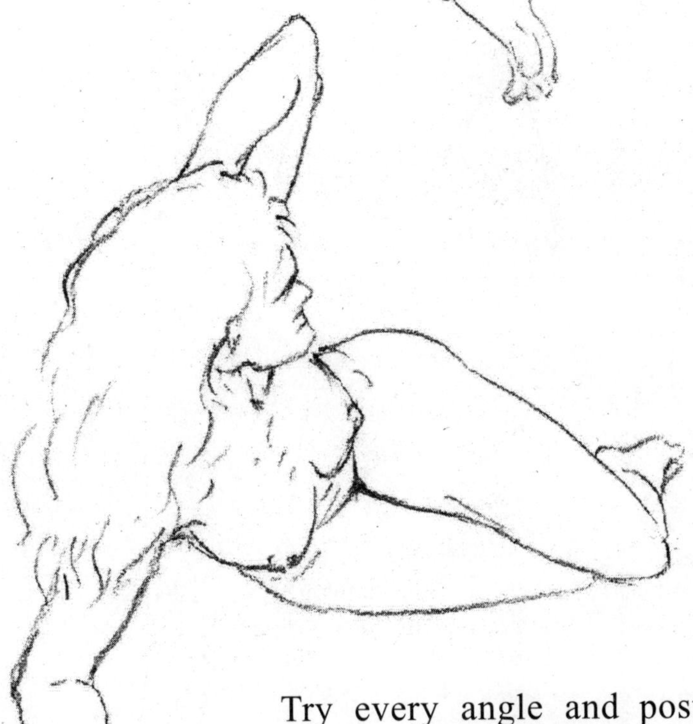

Try every angle and posture so that you can get familiar with the different changes you may have to face with the changing positions.

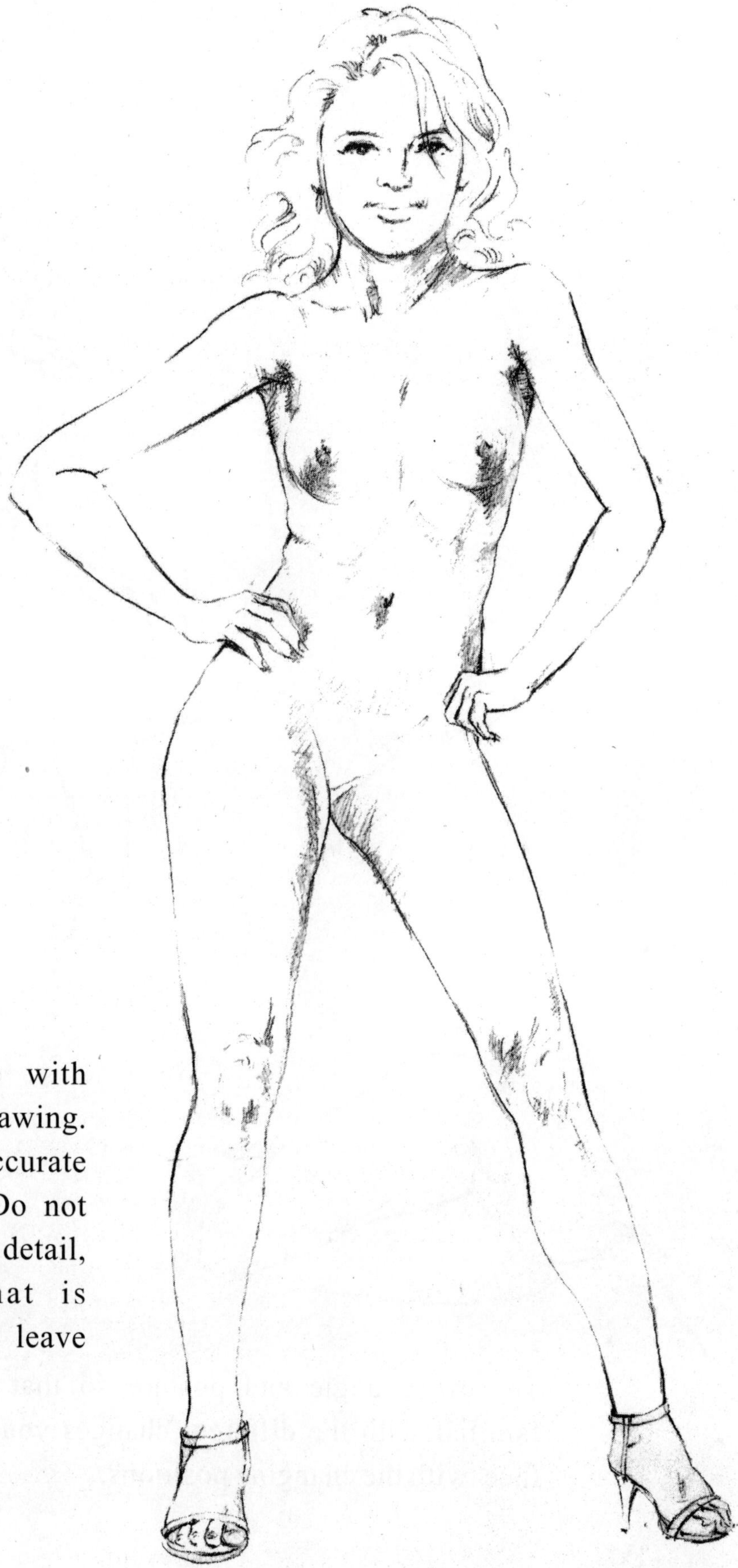

Now practise with single line drawing. It should be accurate and precise. Do not add too much detail, stick to what is necessary and leave the rest.

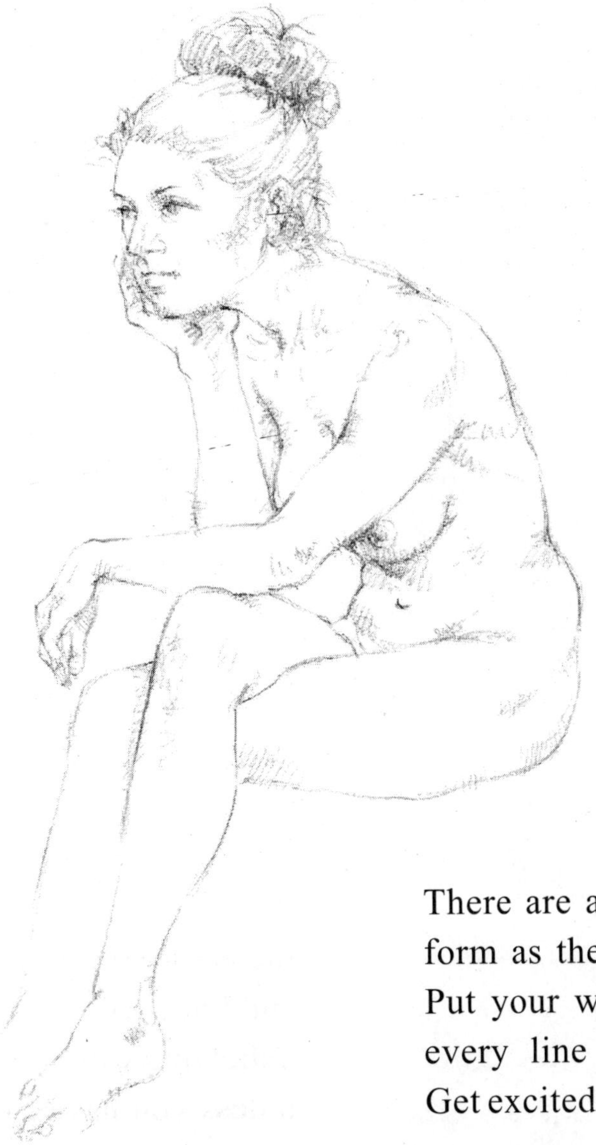

There are as many ways to interpret form as there are forms to interpret. Put your whole mind and body into every line and smudge you make. Get excited. It is really fun.

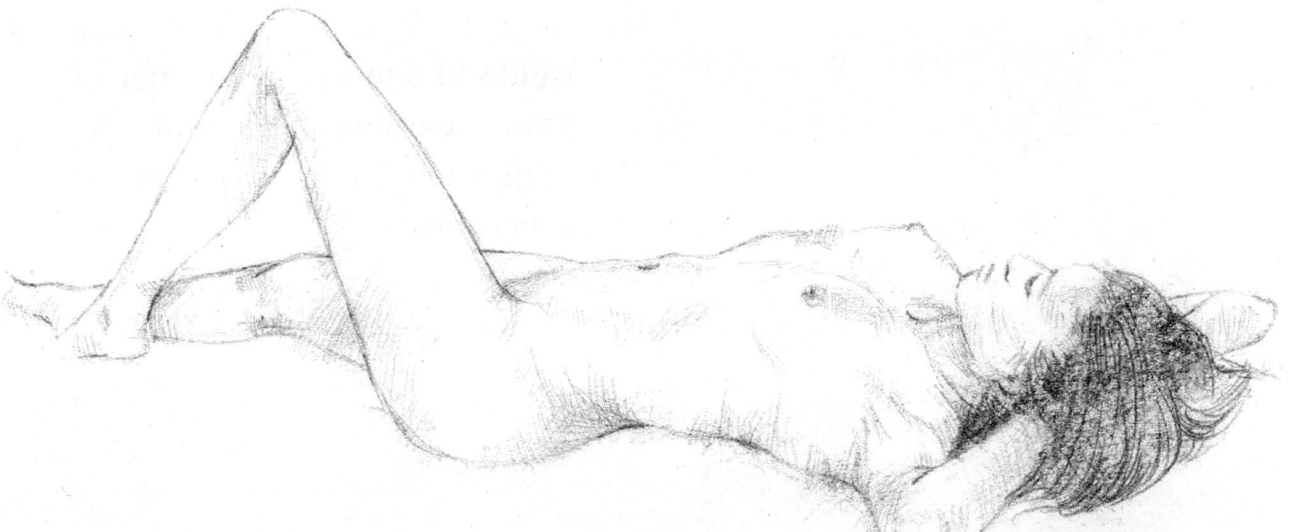

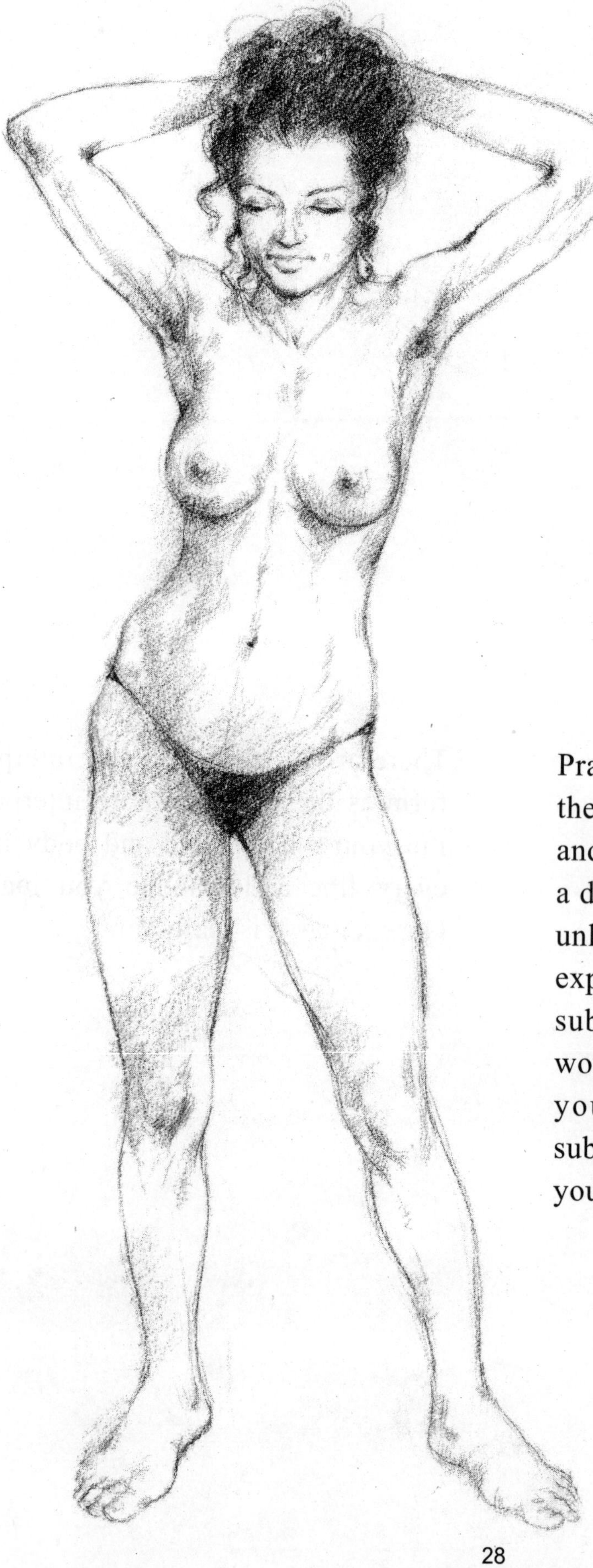

Practise regularly because it is the only way to get experience and knowledge. The language of a drawing can not be understood unless you have a good working experience of the choice of your subject. What and how you would like to use is a matter of your temperament and the subject matter, an experiment of your choice.

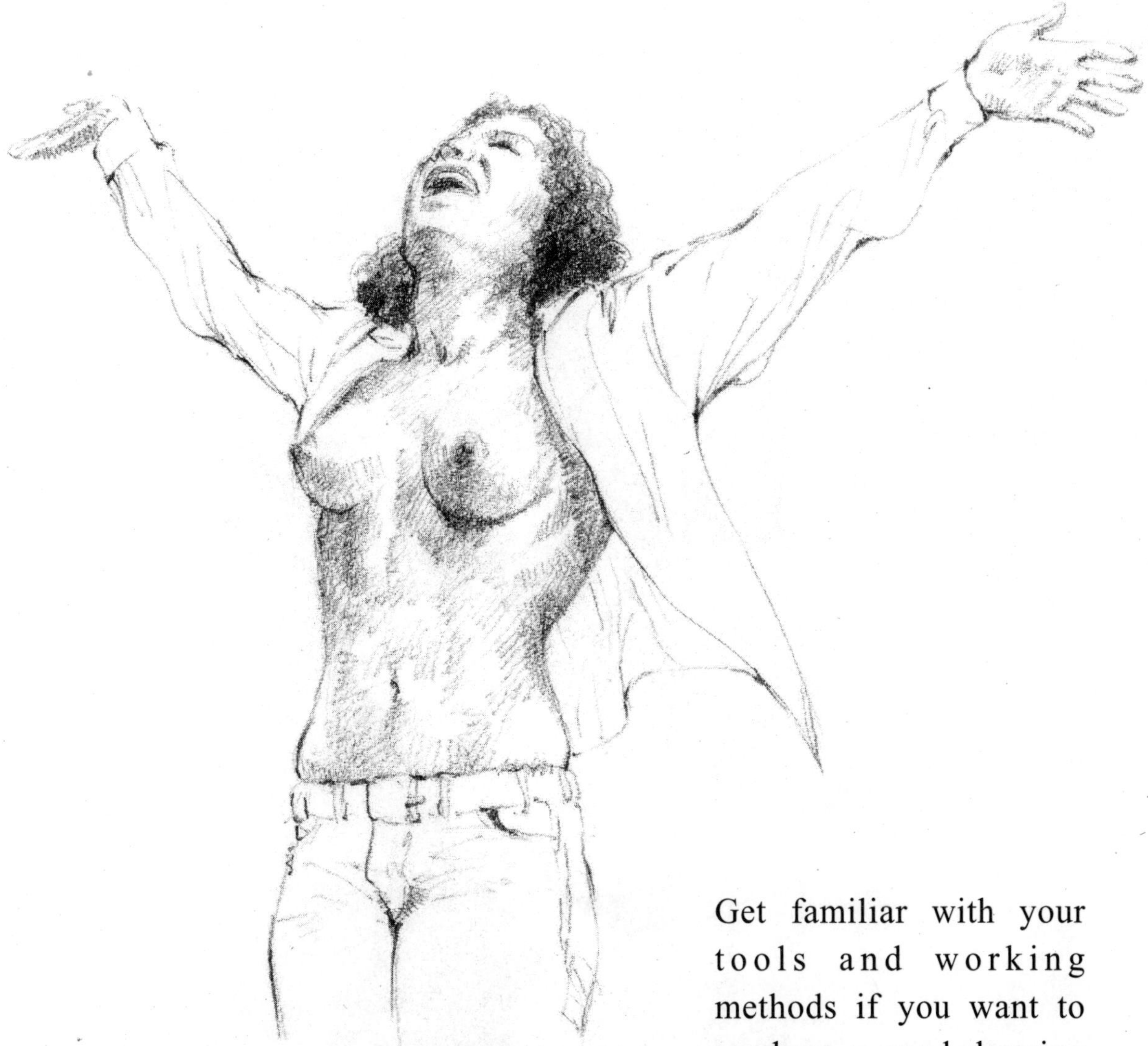

Get familiar with your tools and working methods if you want to produce a good drawing of female figures.

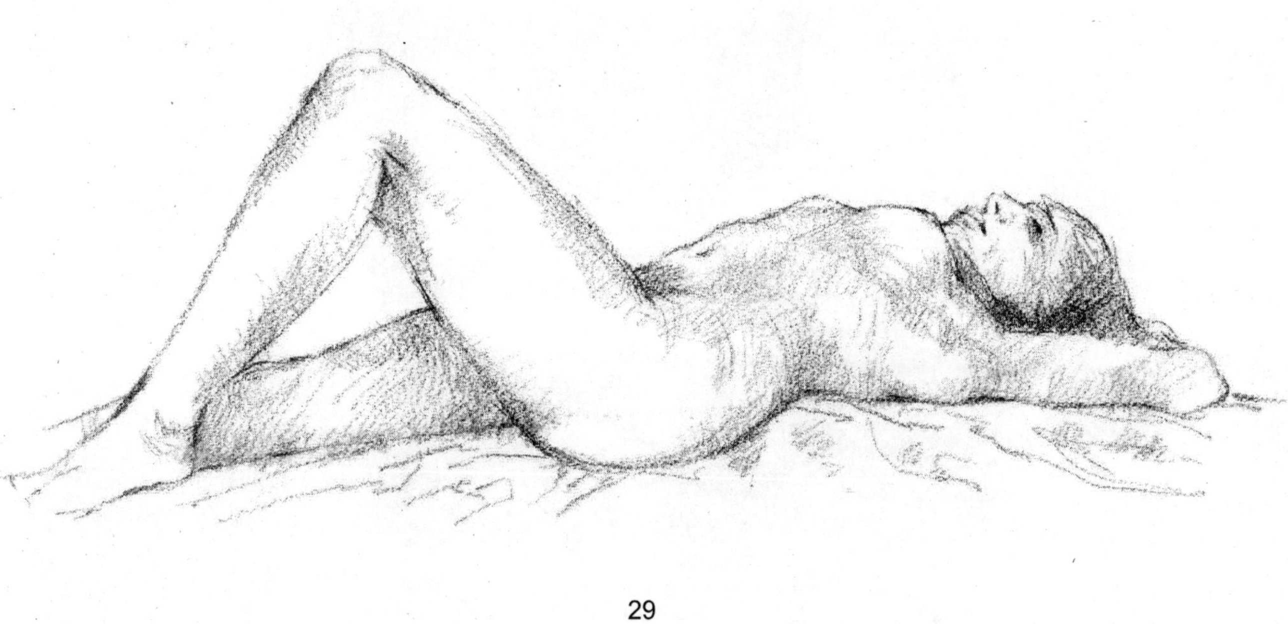

Do not just copy a photograph, interpret the figure as per your view and inclination. Decide on what you are going to use and put the rest out of reach.

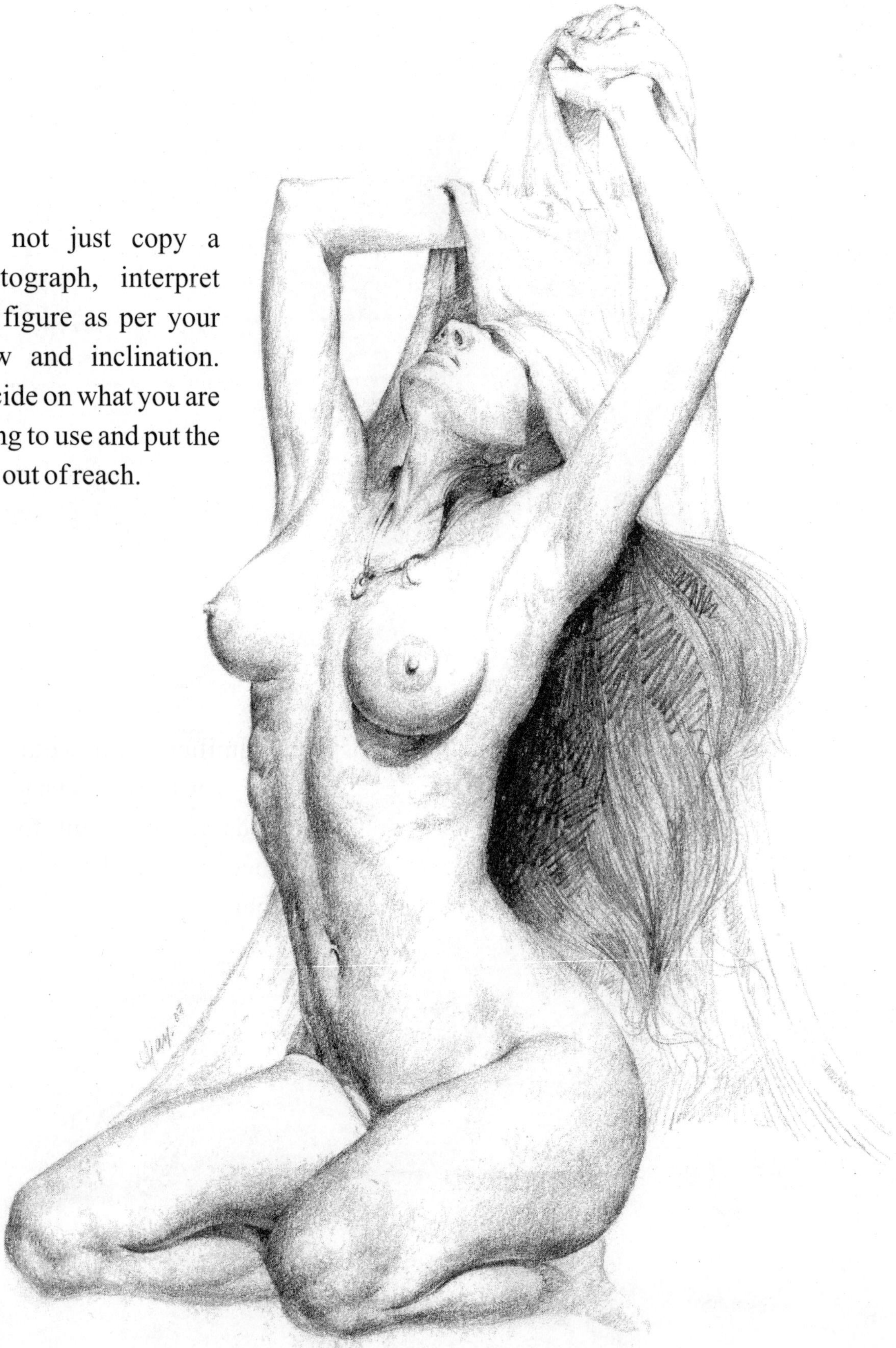

Once you get control on your pencil then the lines are like melodies. You can play and enjoy them as and when you wish.

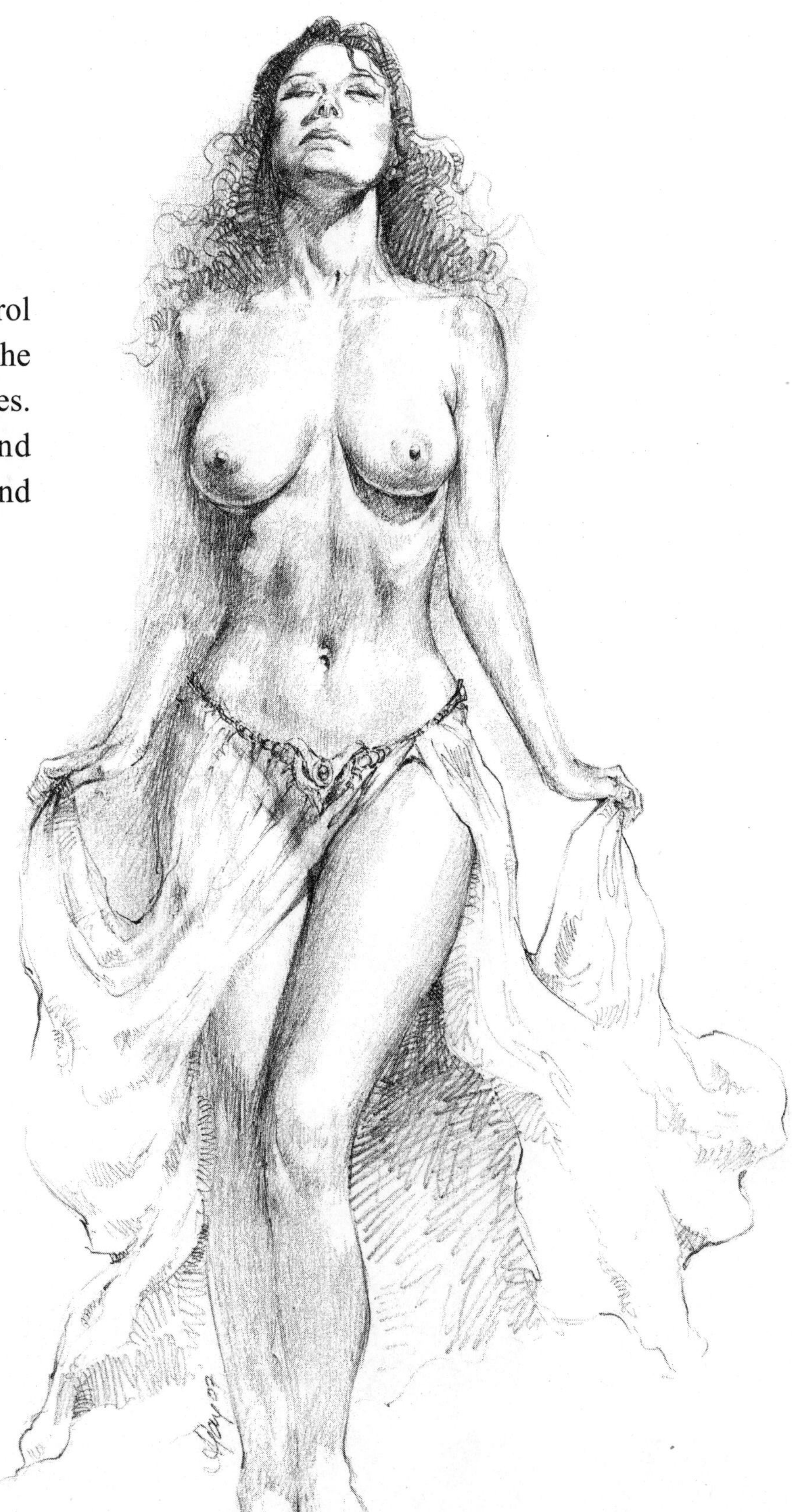

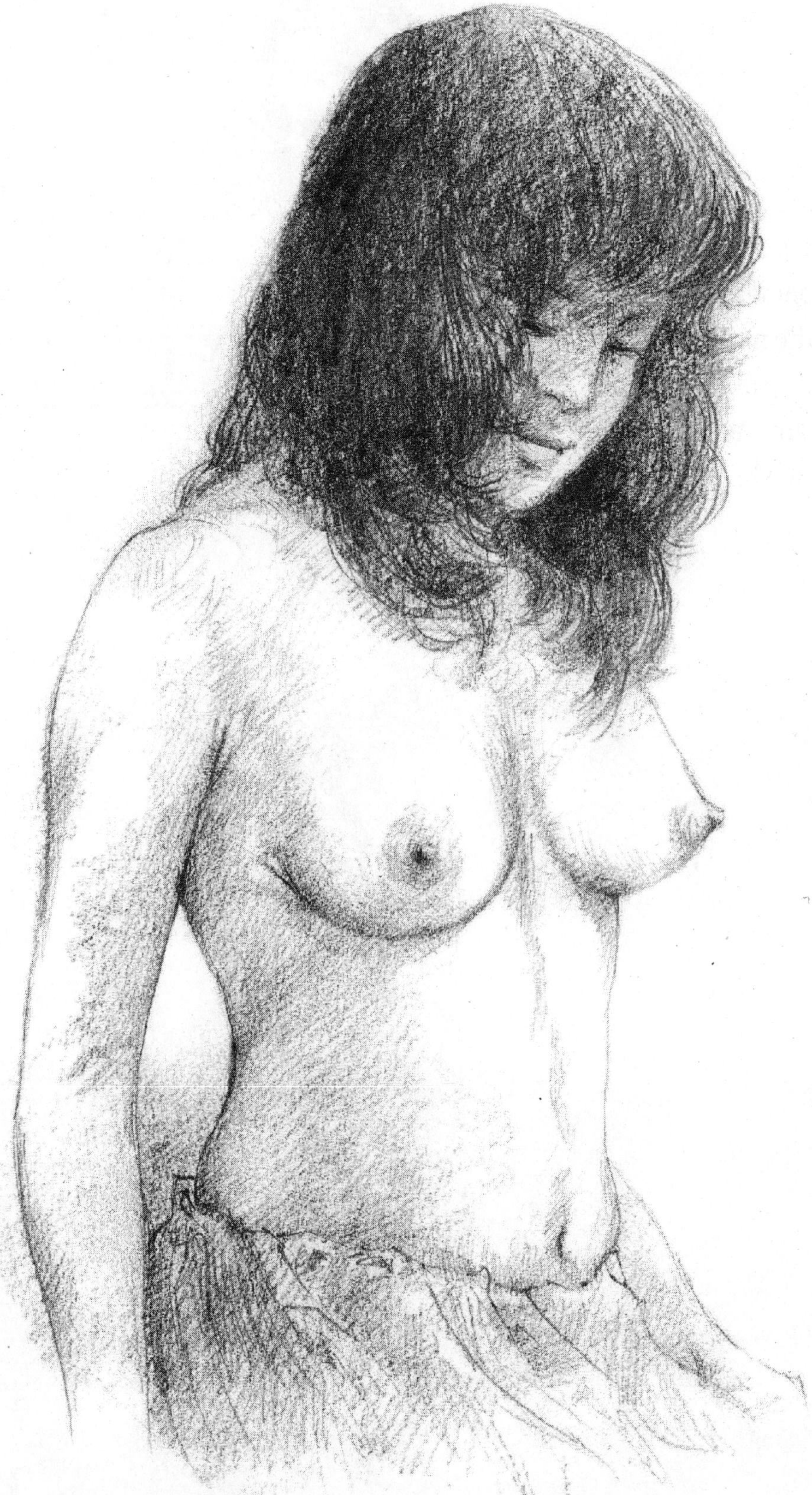

If you really want to learn sketching, I would always recommend drawing directly from life. The subject of your sketch should be in the process of doing something. Look at this girl, the back view is as much sensual as any front view would be. Excellent curvatures are developed by a very simple walking posture. The lifted right leg makes this happen.

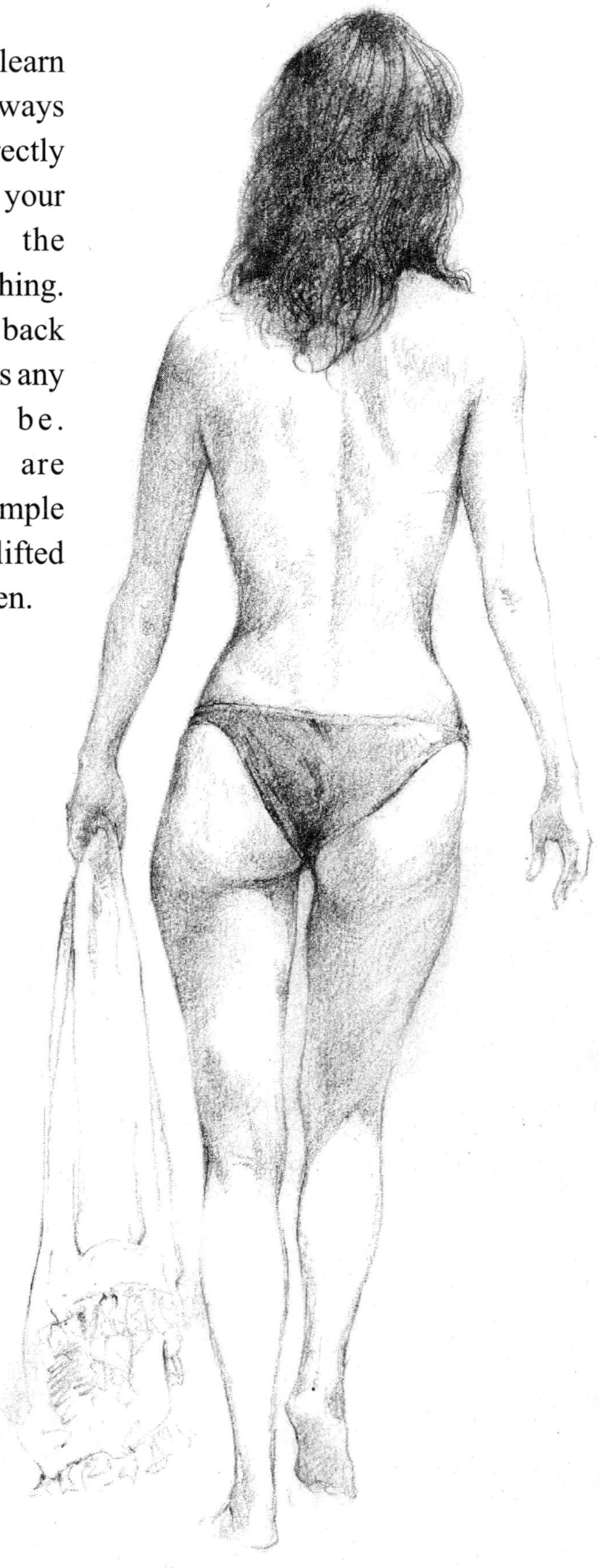

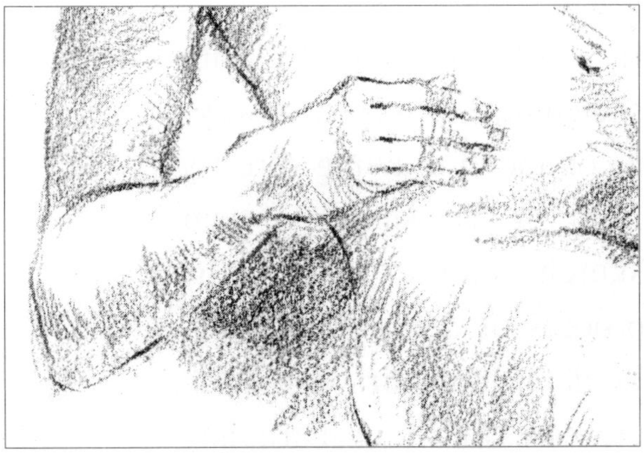

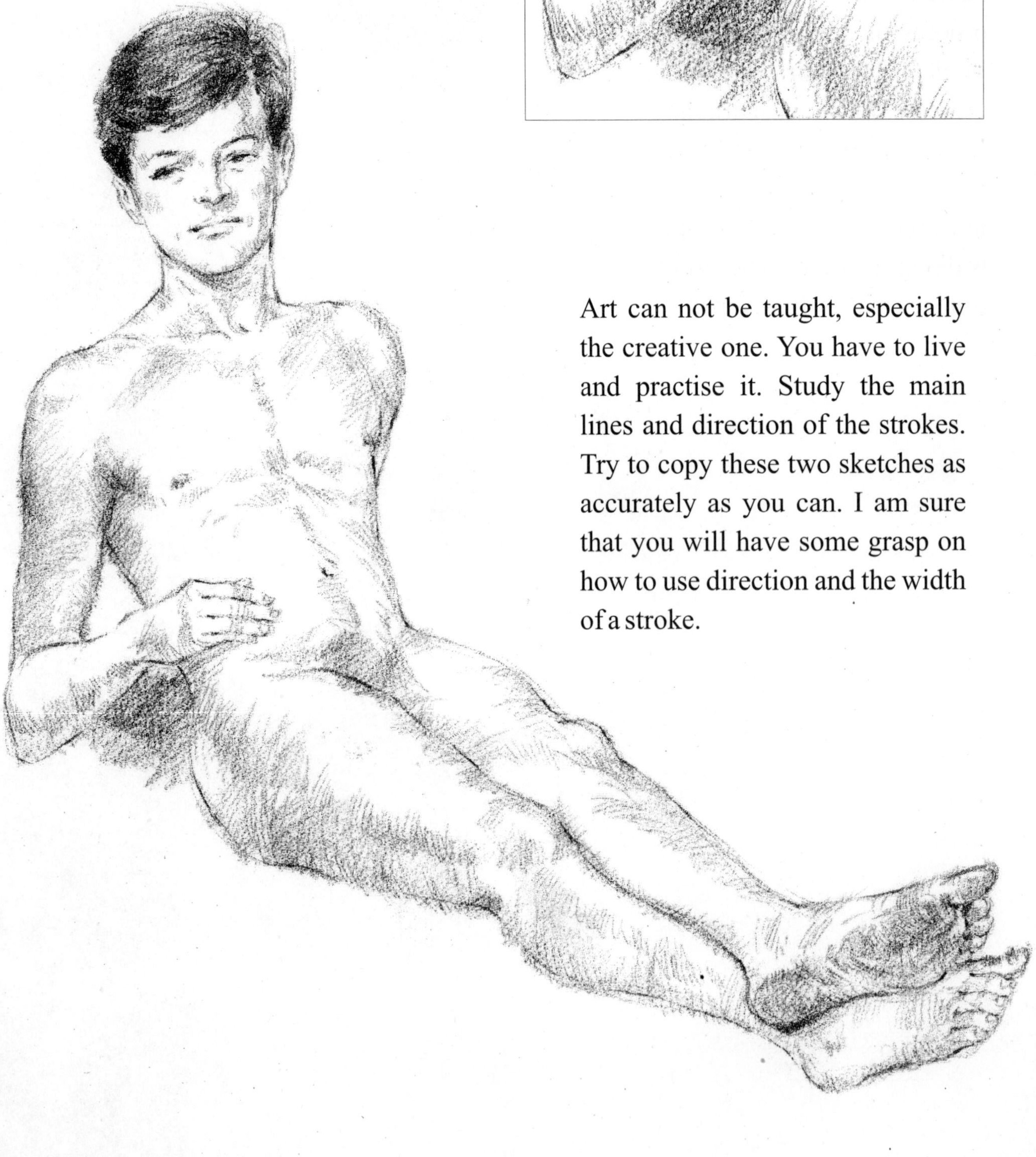

Art can not be taught, especially the creative one. You have to live and practise it. Study the main lines and direction of the strokes. Try to copy these two sketches as accurately as you can. I am sure that you will have some grasp on how to use direction and the width of a stroke.

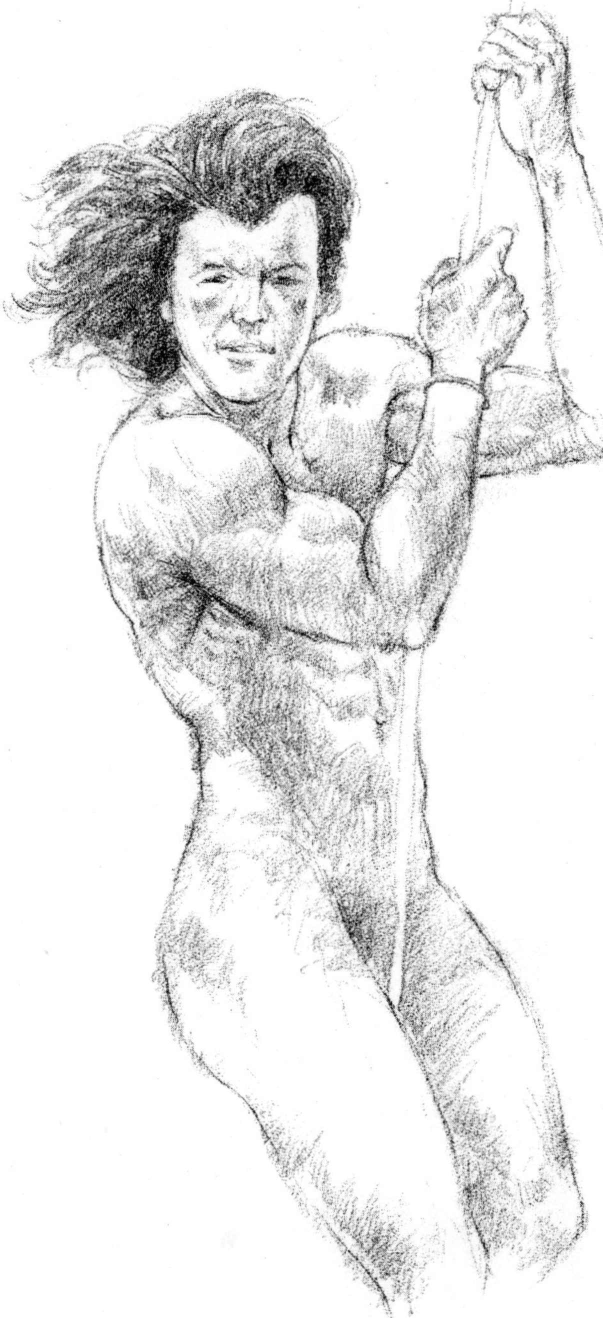

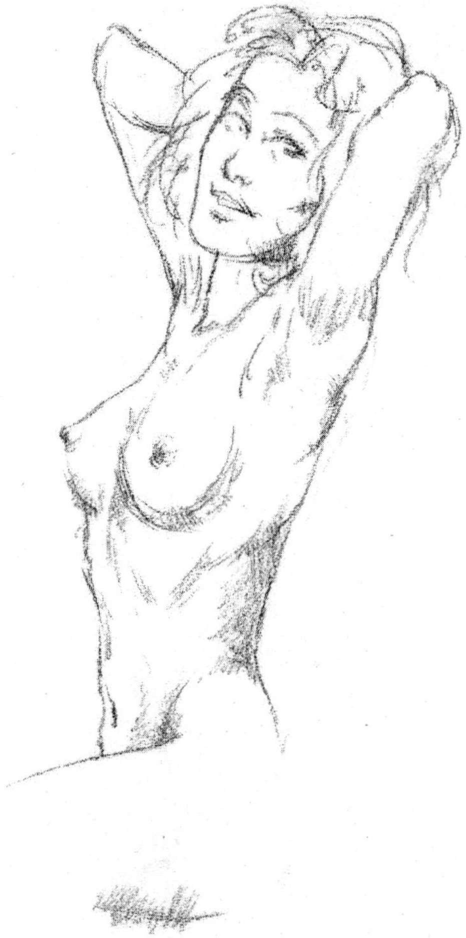

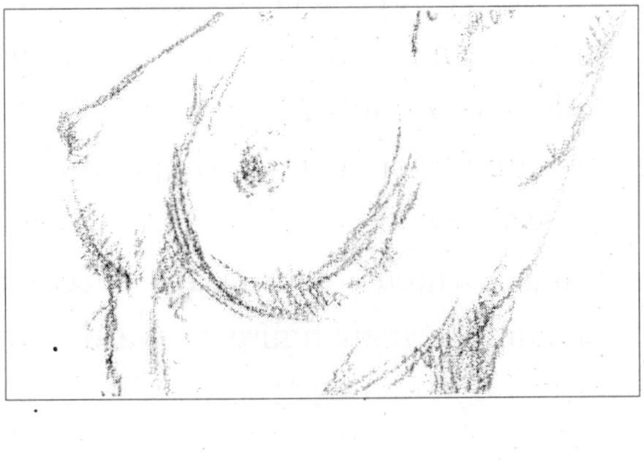

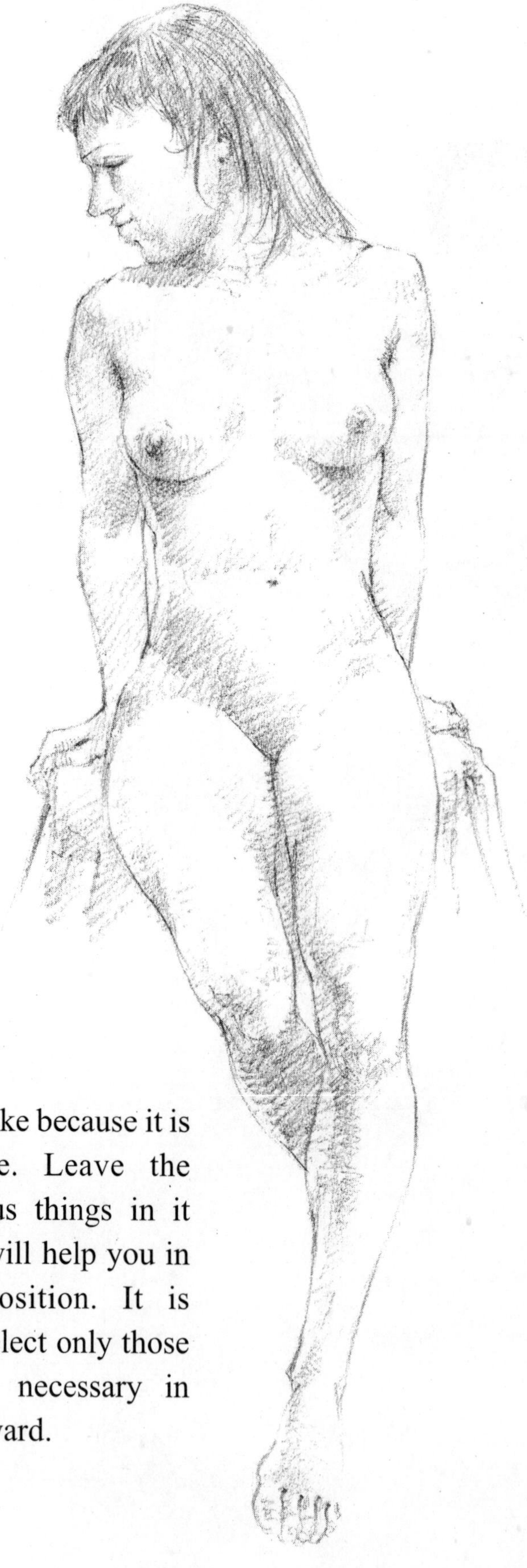

Draw the way you feel and like because it is a matter of your choice. Leave the background and the various things in it unless you think that they will help you in producing a good composition. It is advisable that you should select only those things which seem really necessary in pushing the main figure forward.

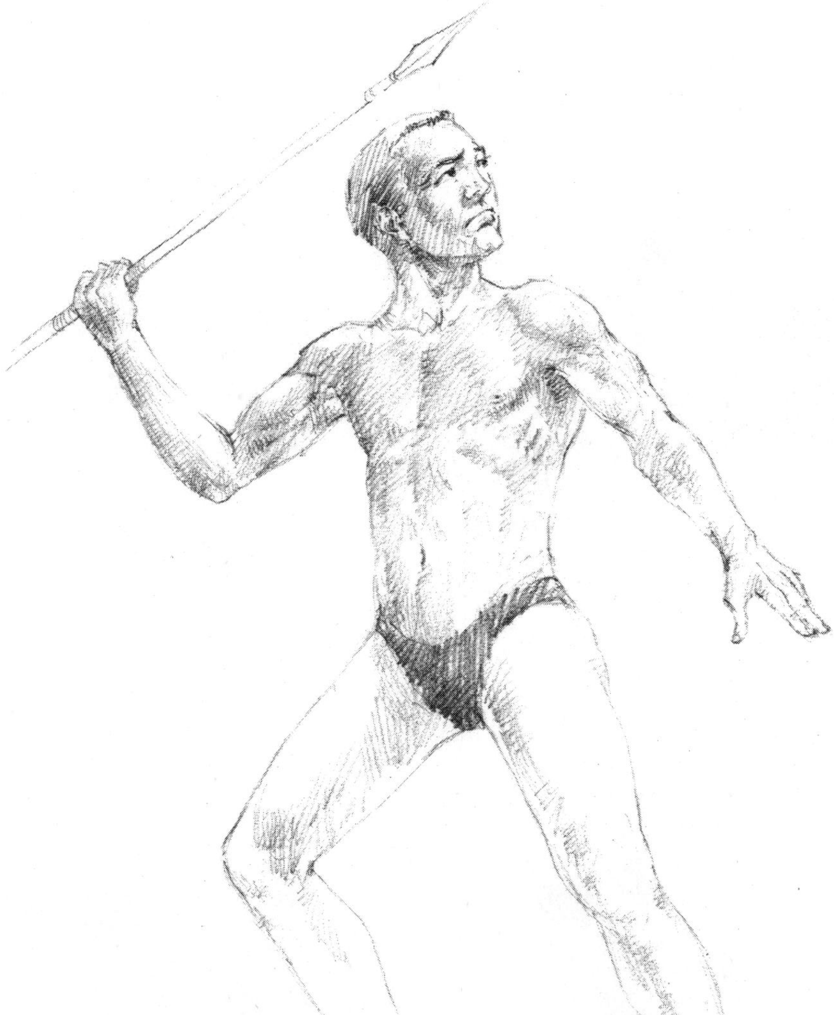

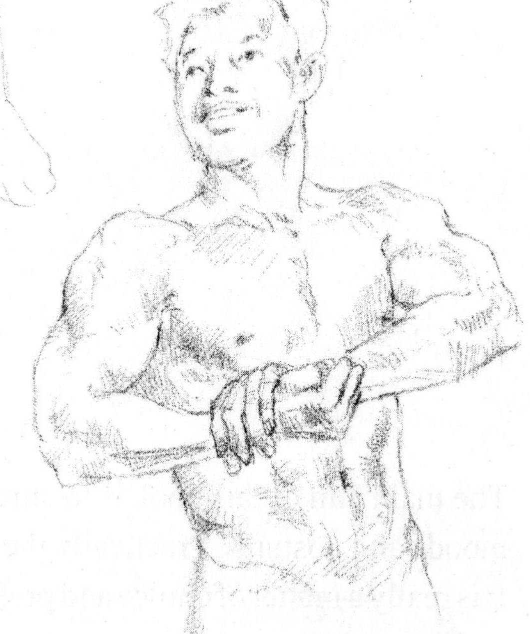

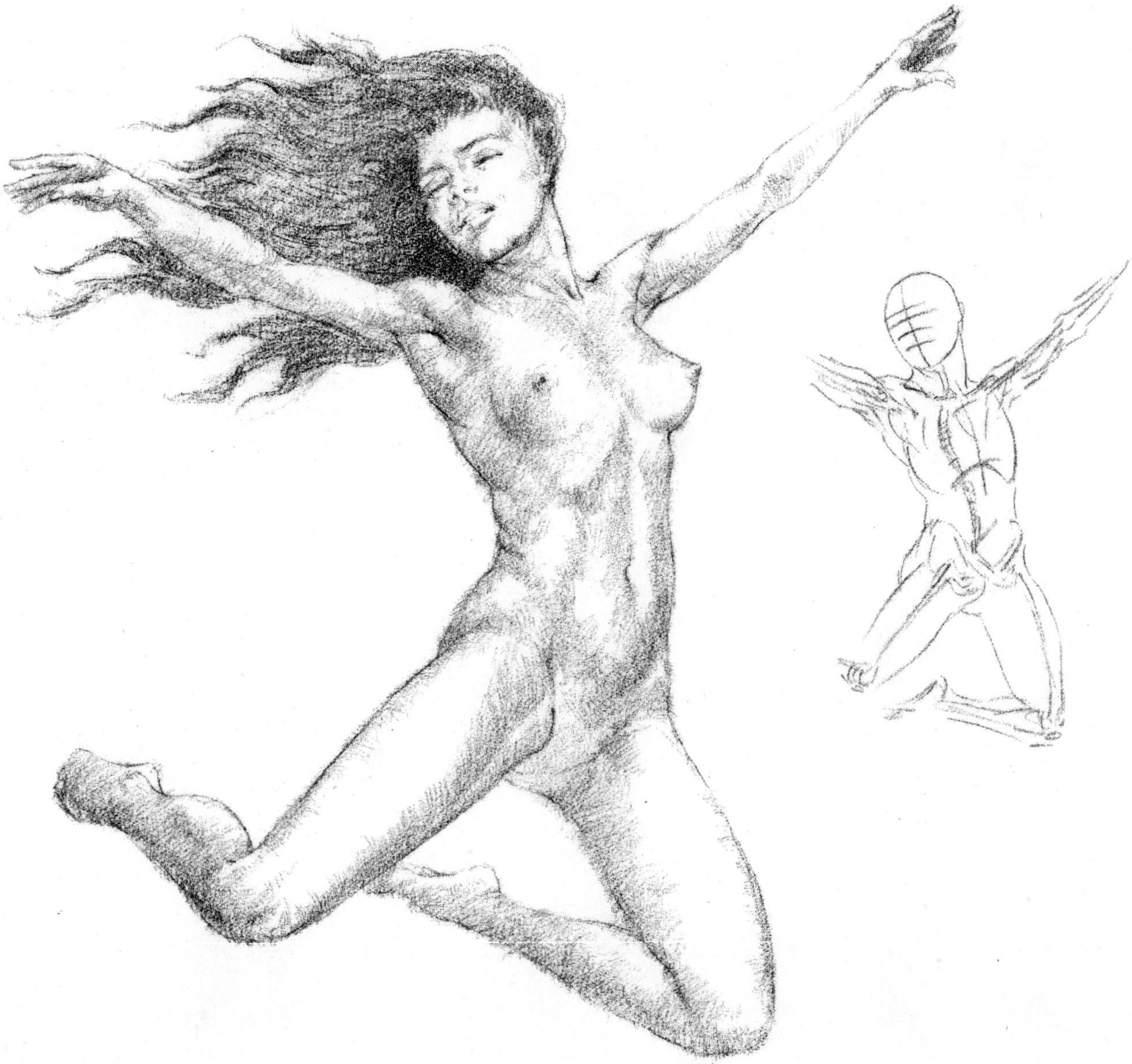

The main aim of this book is to stimulate your interest in drawing the figure in various moods and postures. Practically there are no set rules or standards for art or for beauty. It is really a matter of choice and preference.

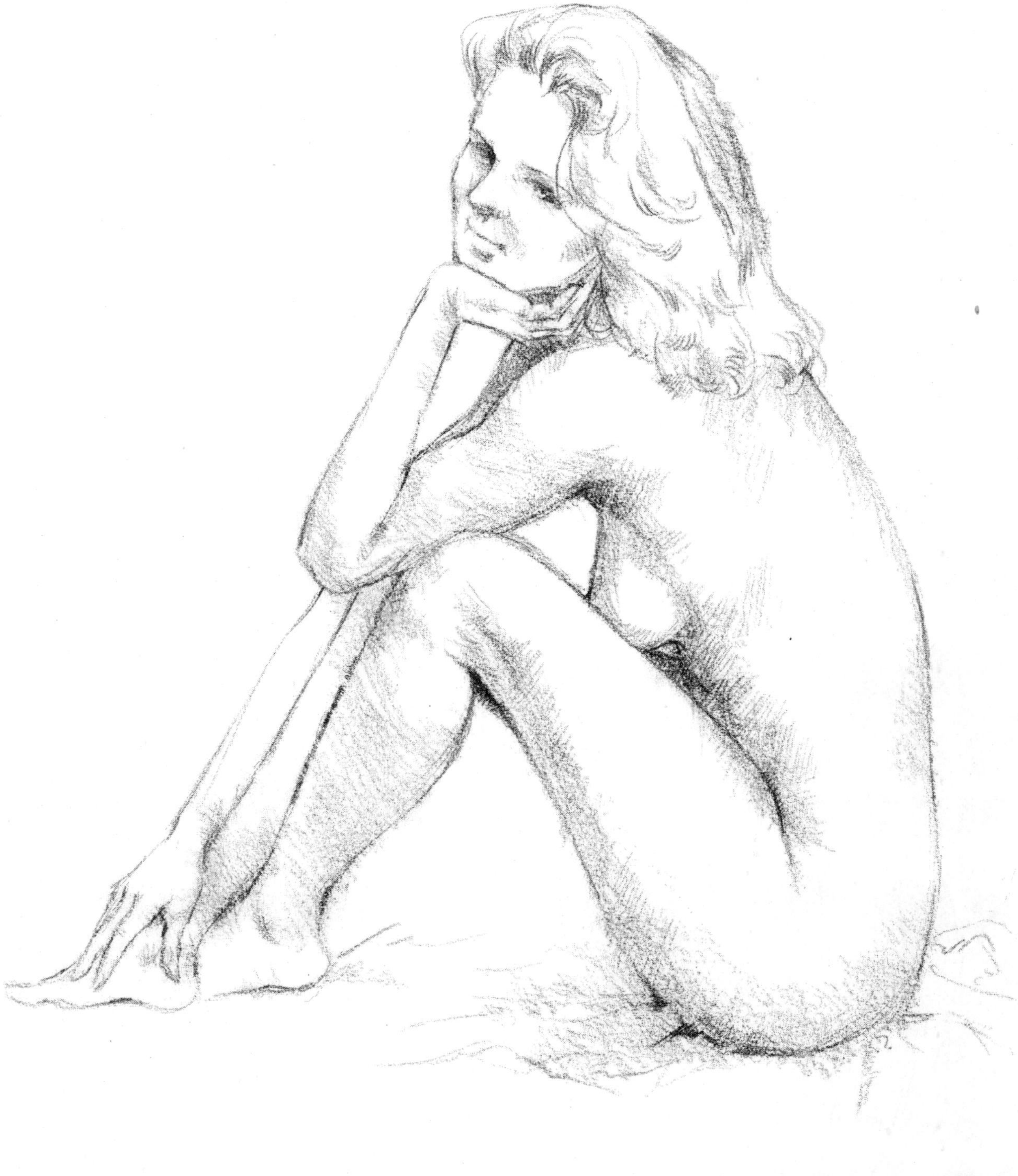

The beautiful proportions, functional grace and never ending variety of a female figure never loses its charm for an artist.

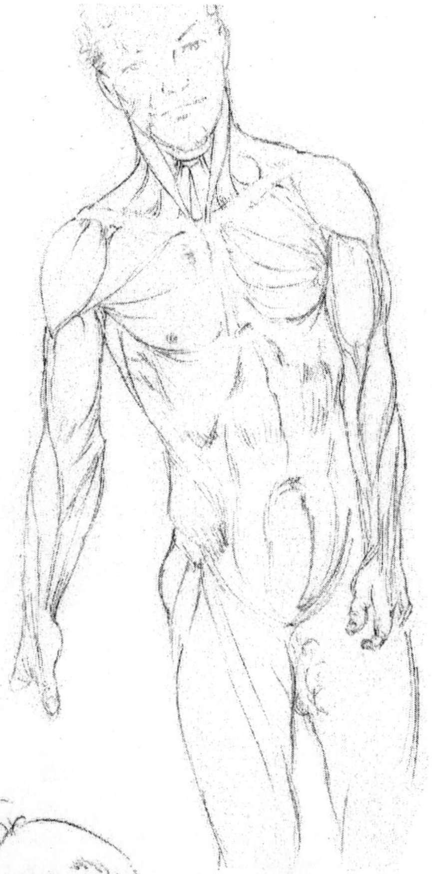

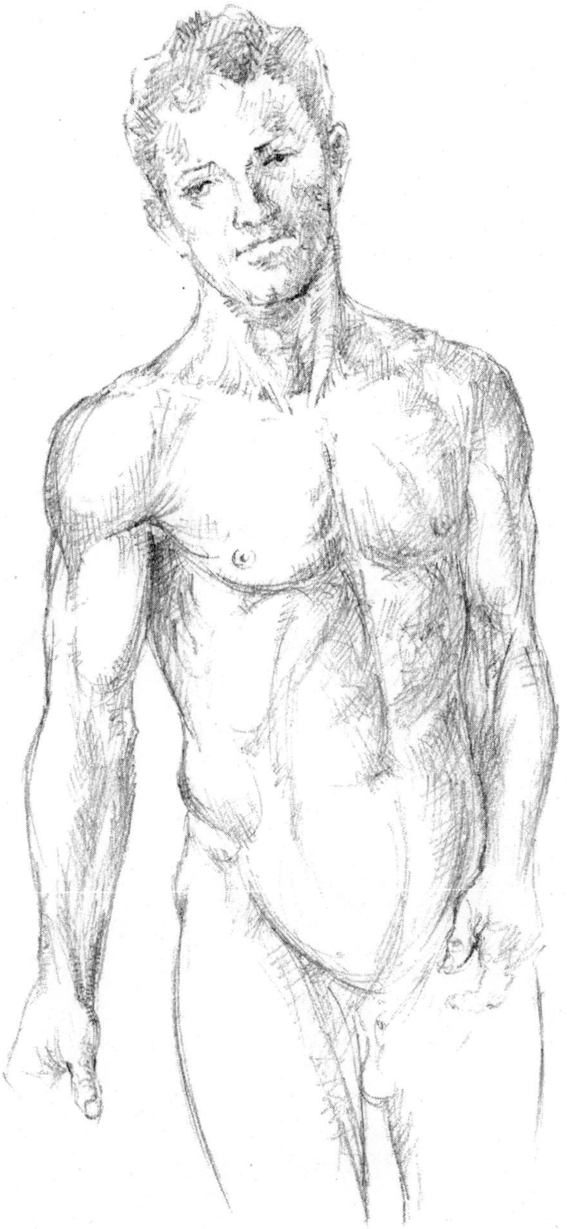

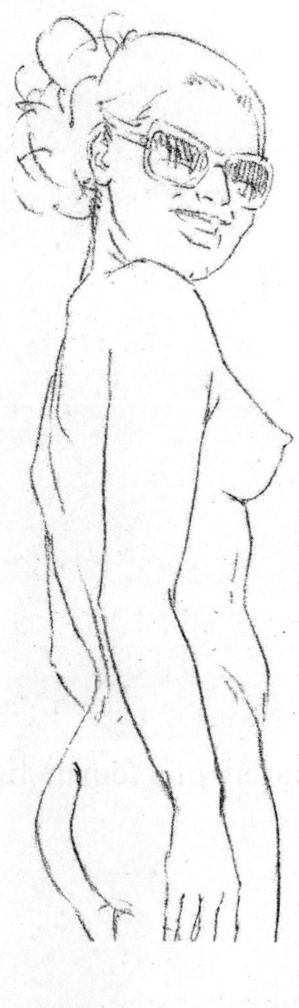

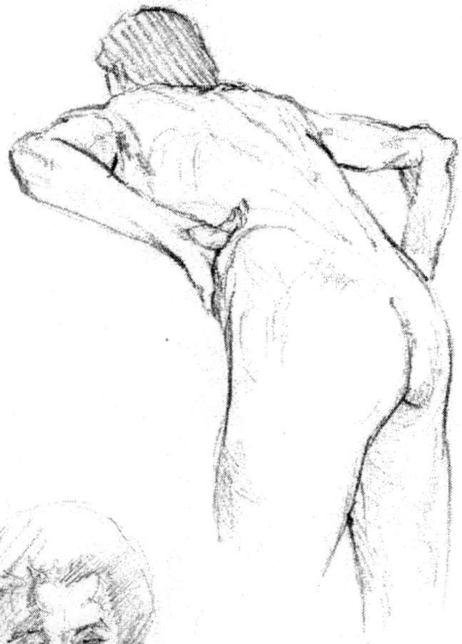

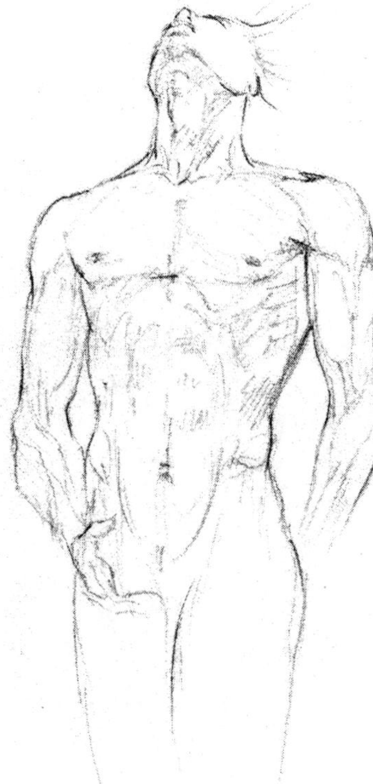

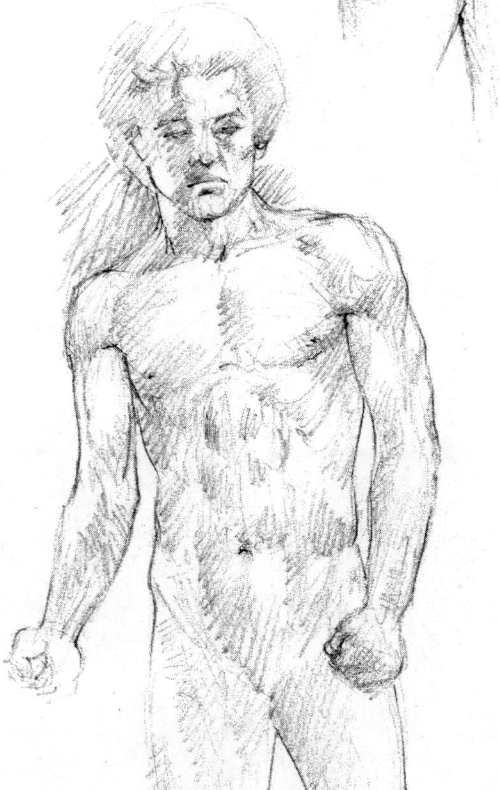

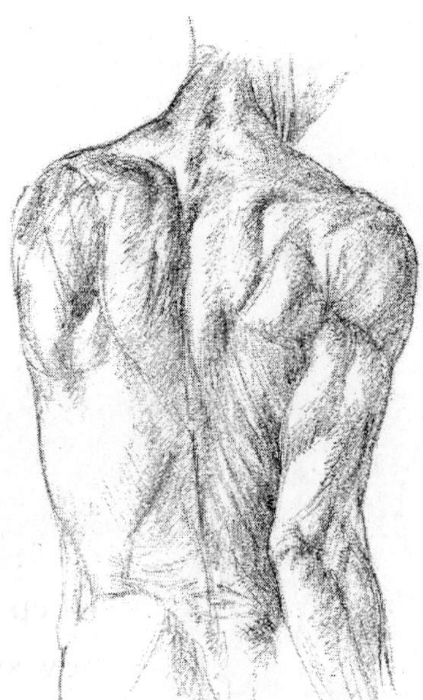

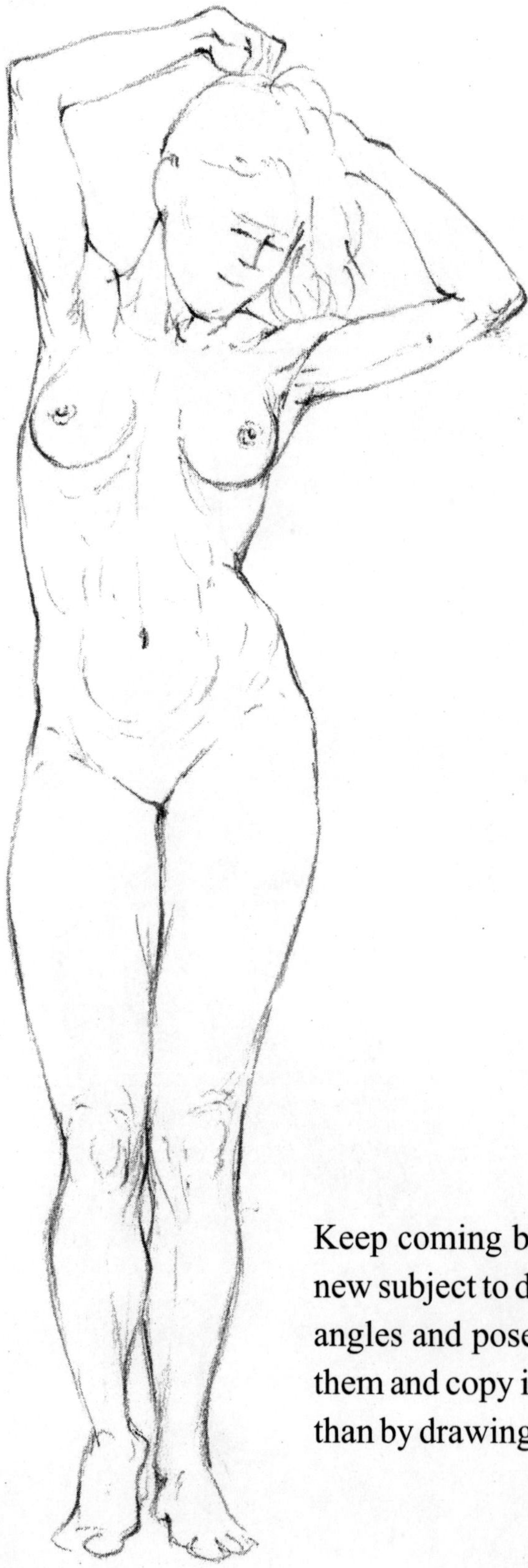

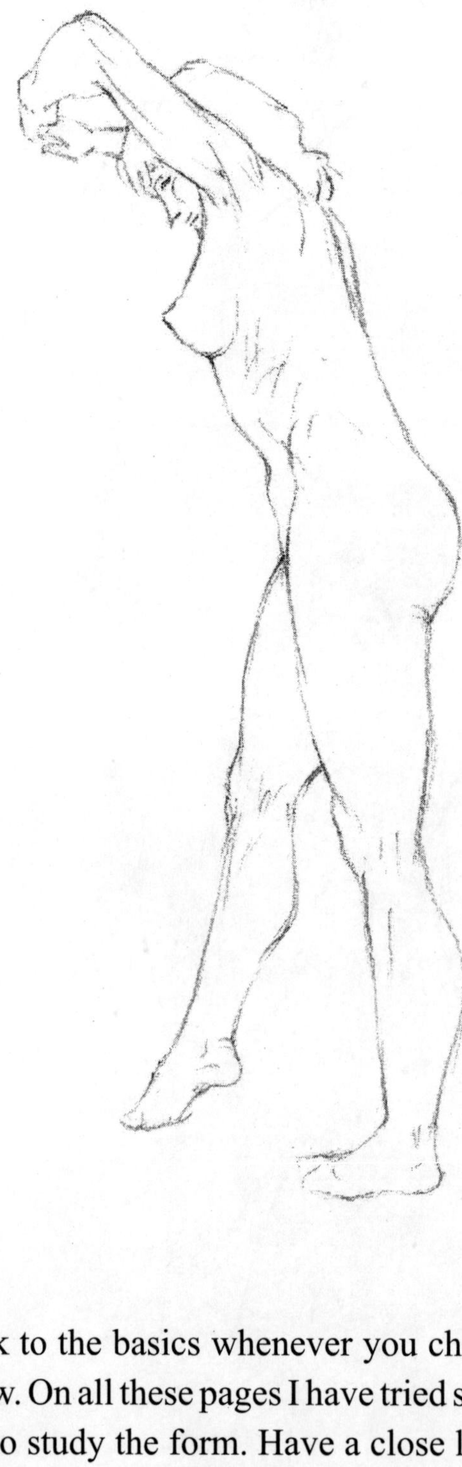

Keep coming back to the basics whenever you choose a new subject to draw. On all these pages I have tried several angles and poses to study the form. Have a close look at them and copy if you like. You will learn more by this way than by drawing a single figure in detail.

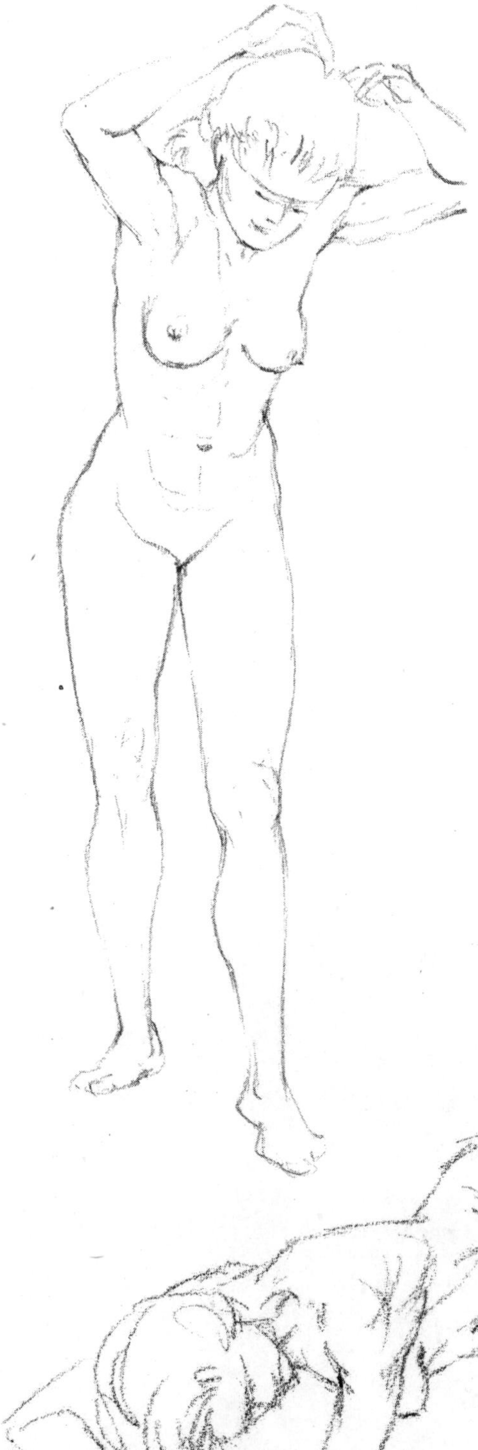

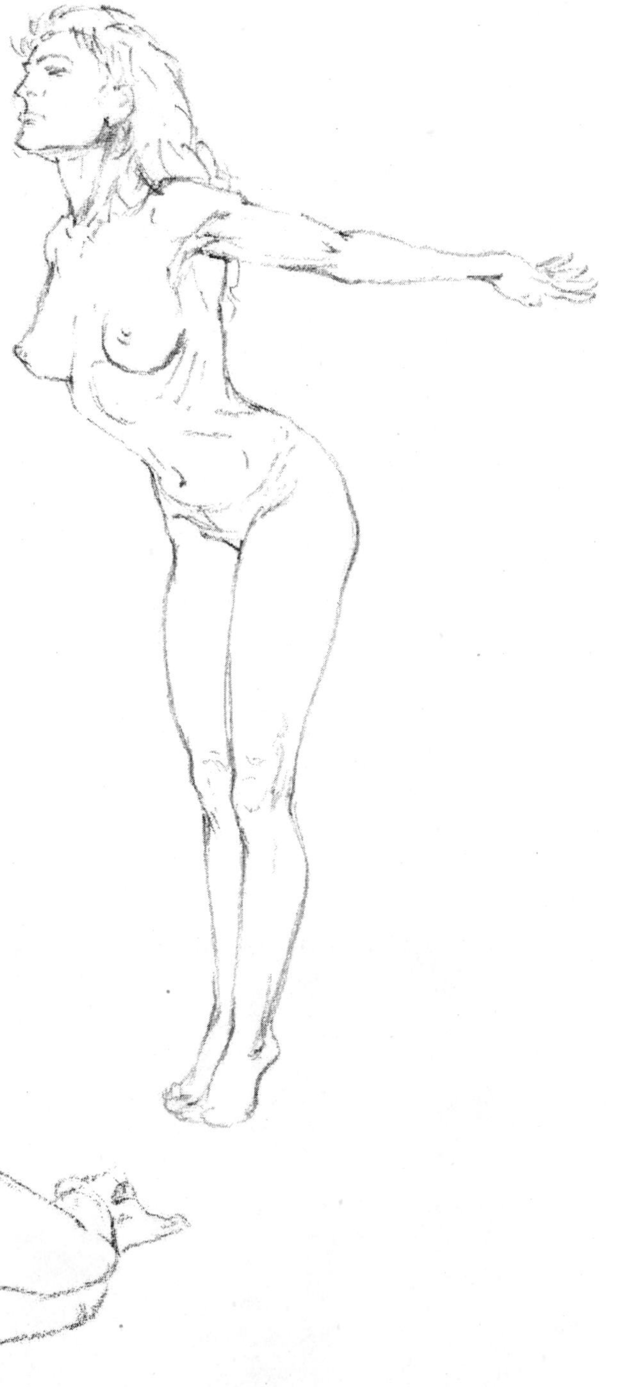

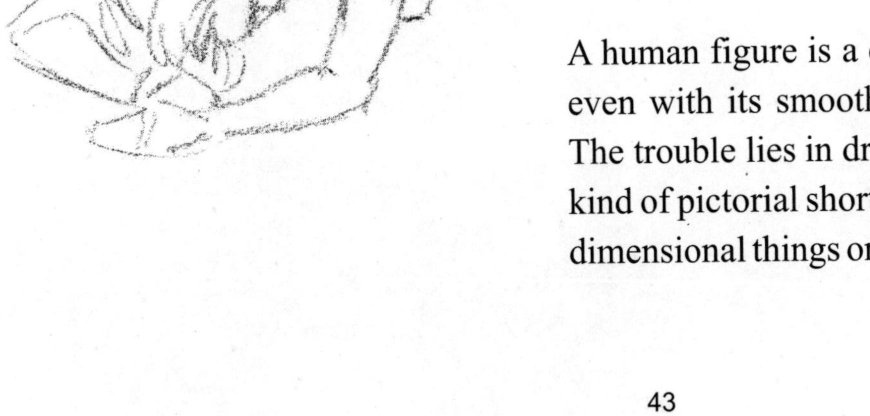

A human figure is a complex structure to draw even with its smooth curvatures and softness. The trouble lies in drawing a sketch, which is a kind of pictorial shorthand used to express three dimensional things on a two dimensional paper.

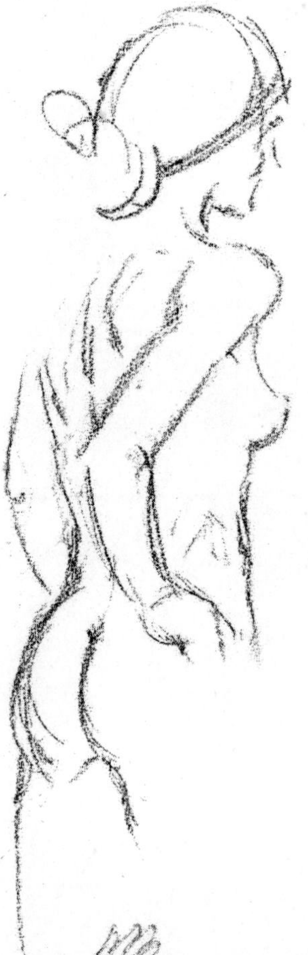

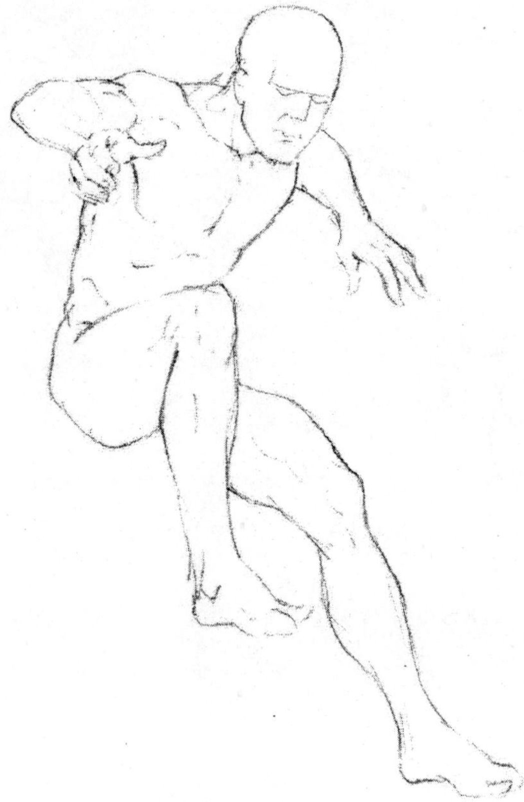

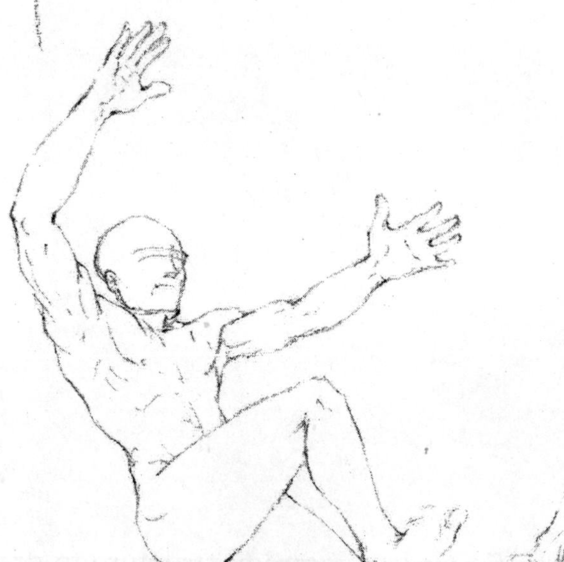

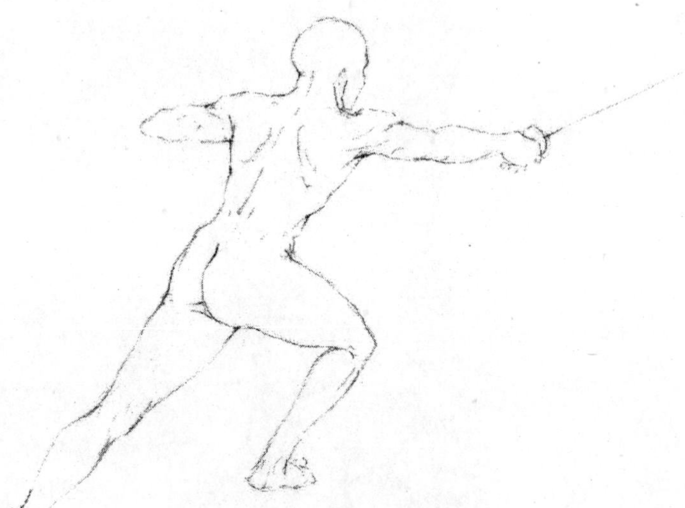

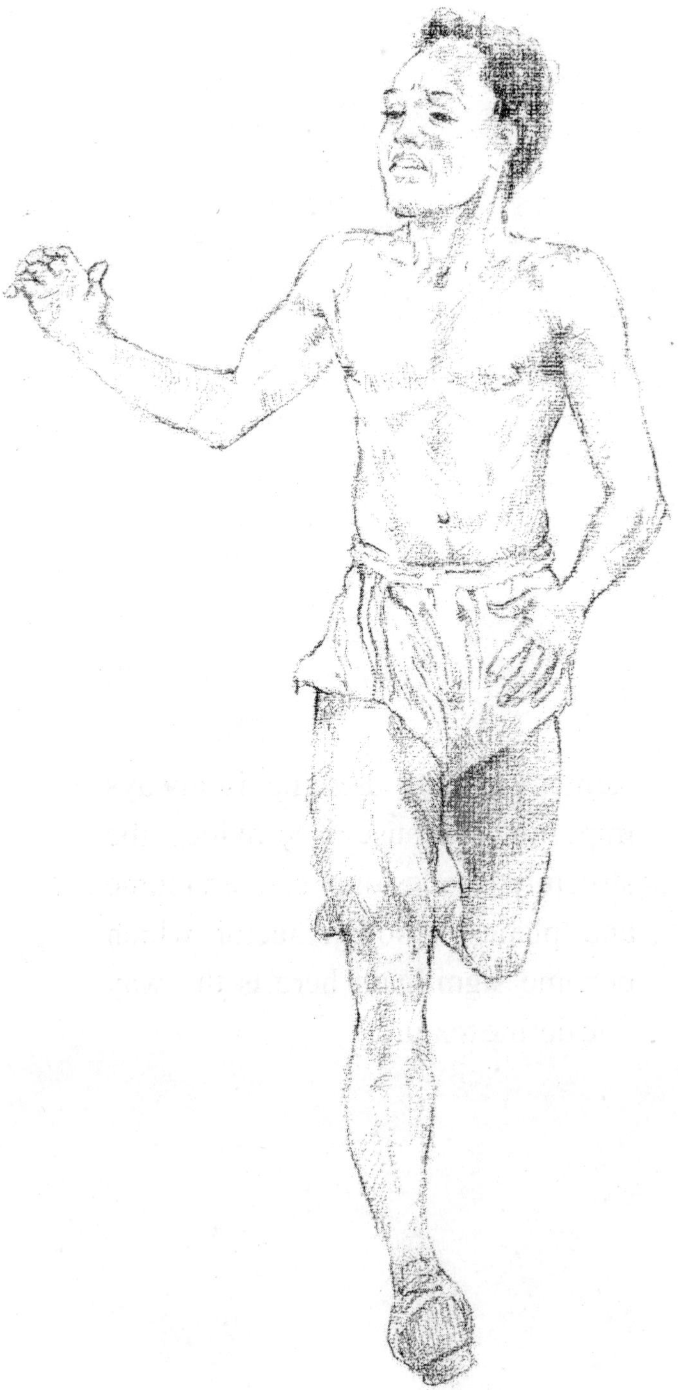

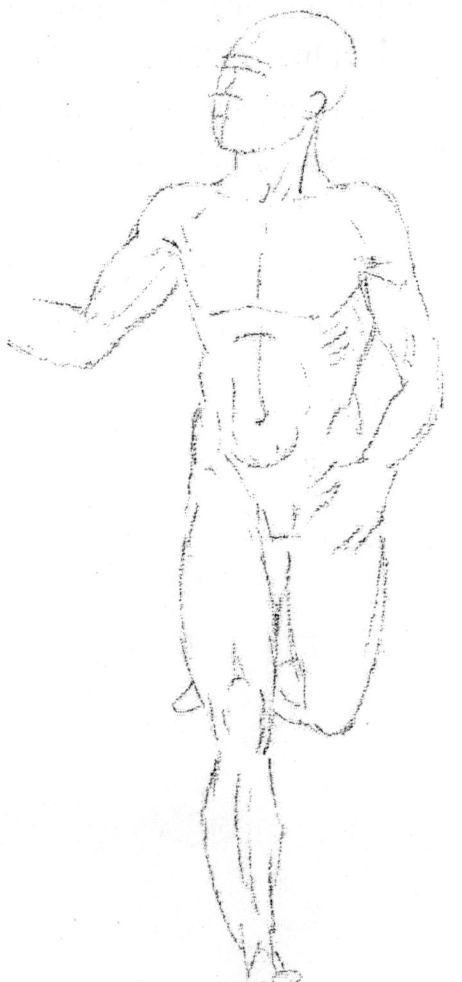

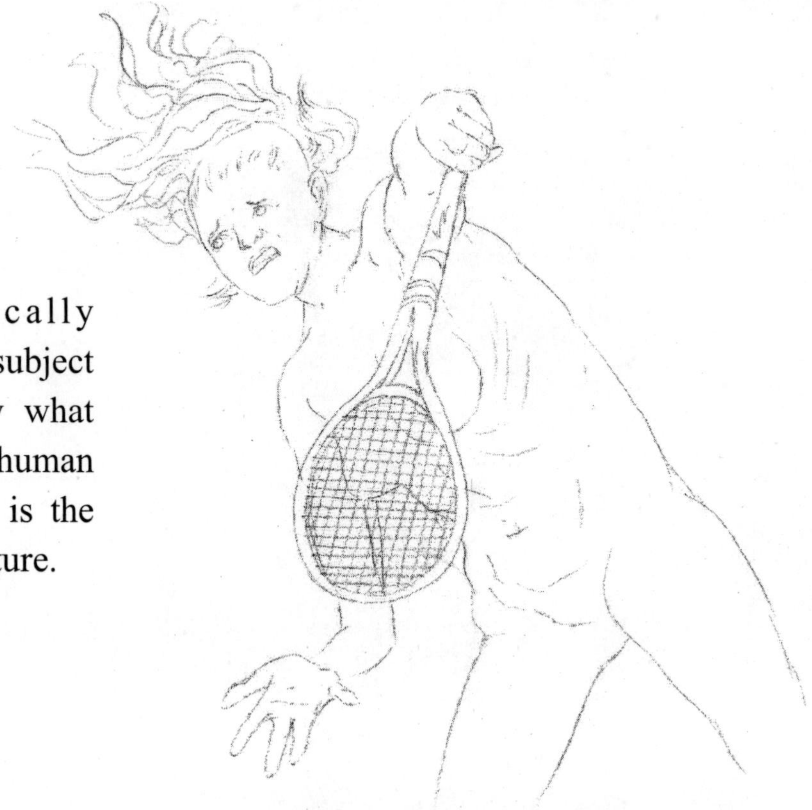

In nature, practically everything is a good subject for drawing. So draw what you like. As far as the human body is concerned, it is the most perfect form in nature.

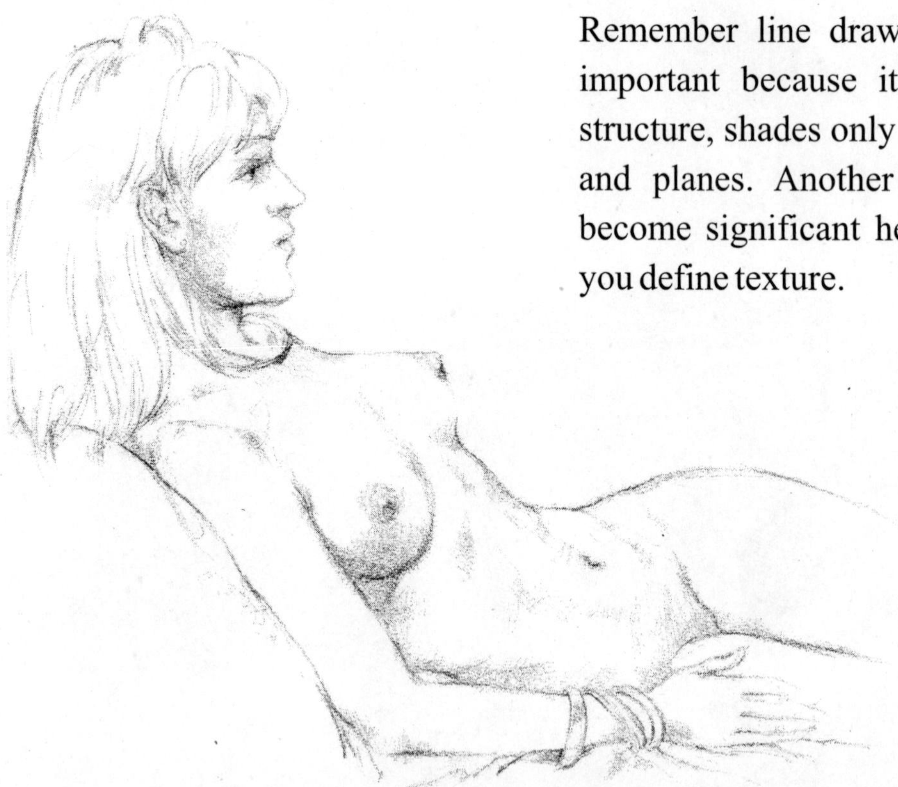

Remember line drawing is always important because it provides the structure, shades only create volume and planes. Another factor which become significant here is the way you define texture.

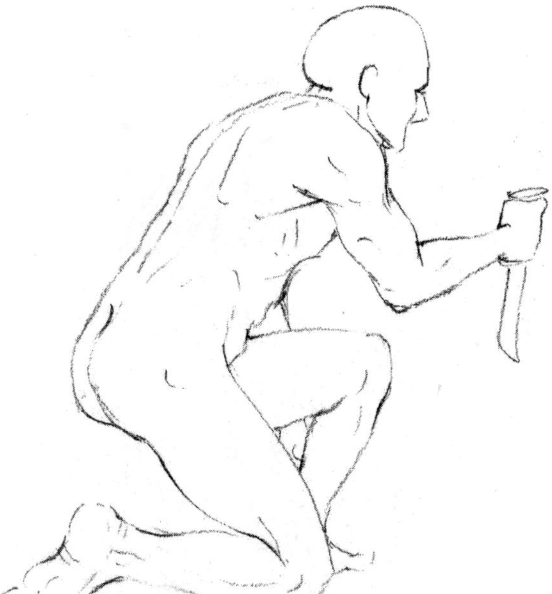

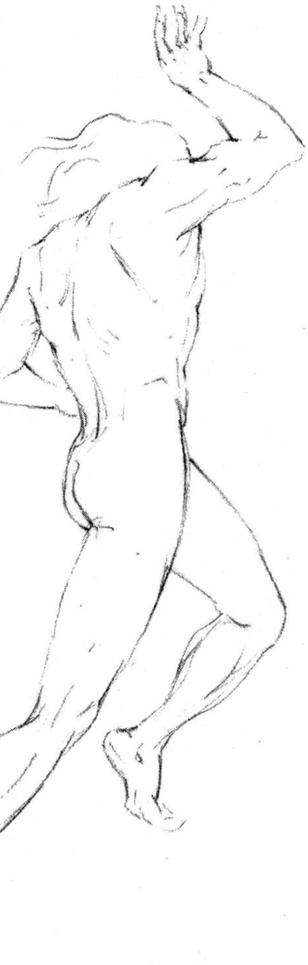

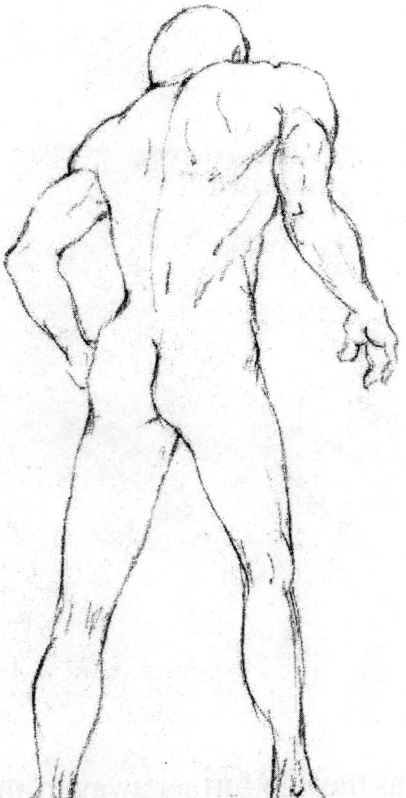

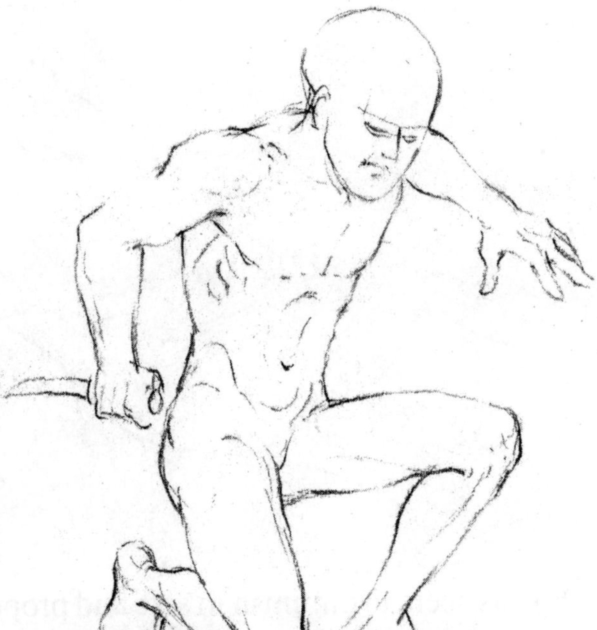

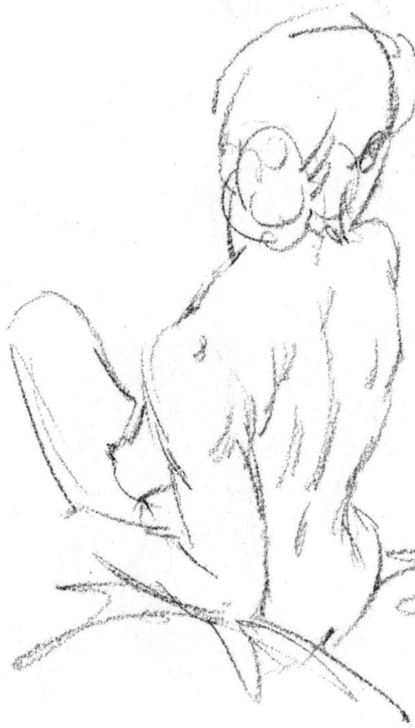

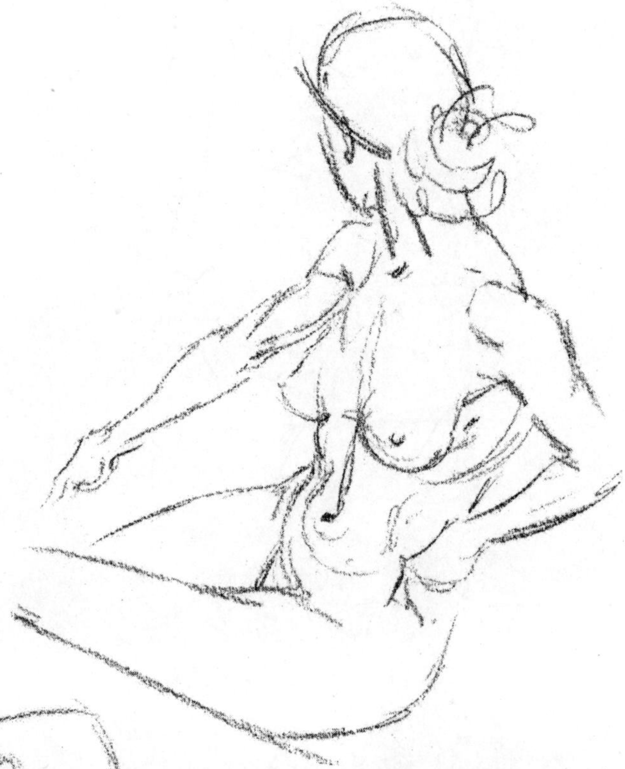

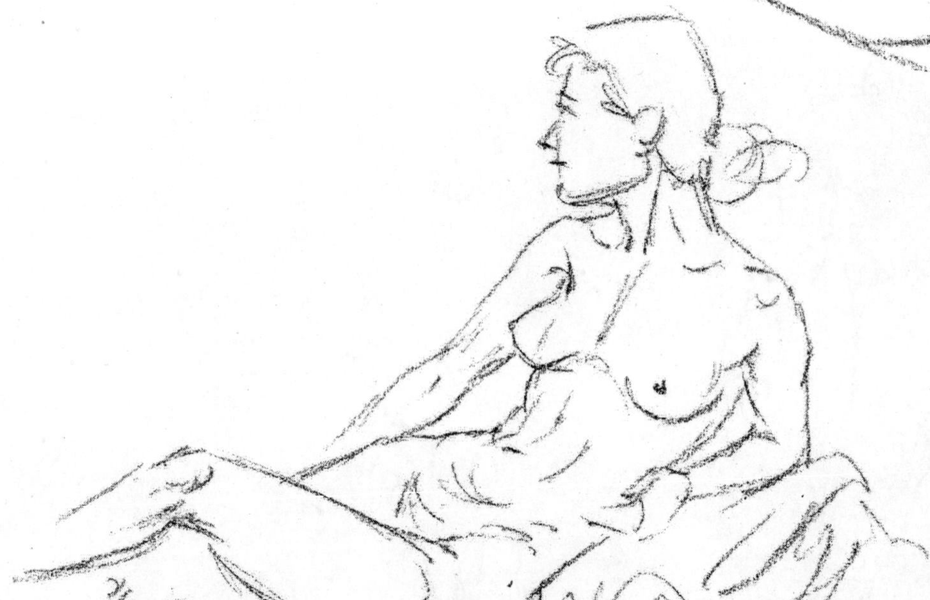

Objects seem to diminish in size and proportion as they go further away from your eyes. If you see the drawings made by the primitive men, you will find that they simply drew the distant objects smaller in size. I would like you to draw all these sketches in as less time as you can, but accurately.

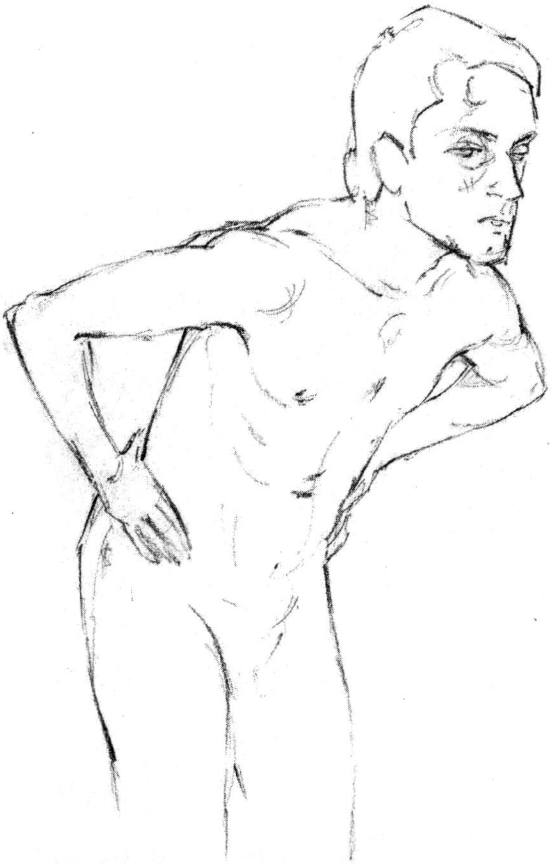

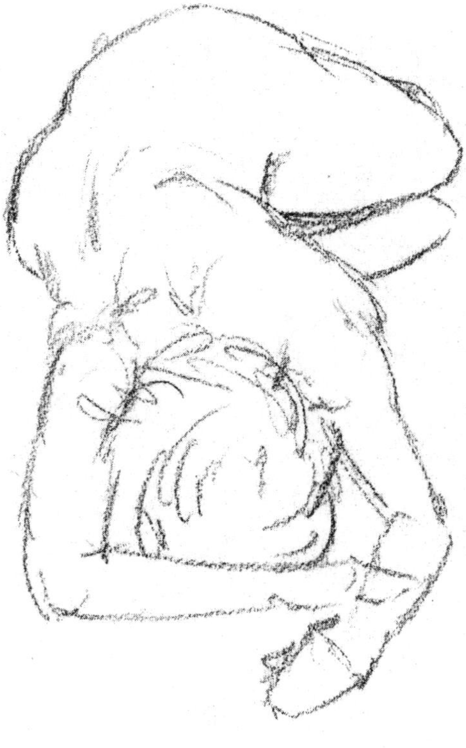

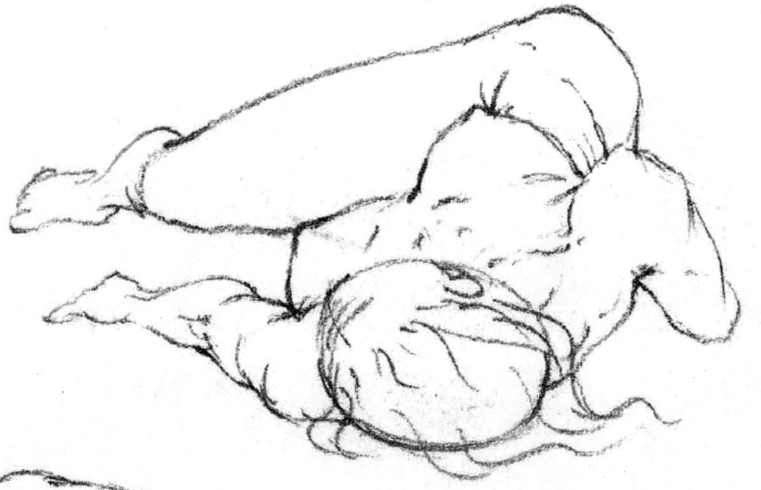

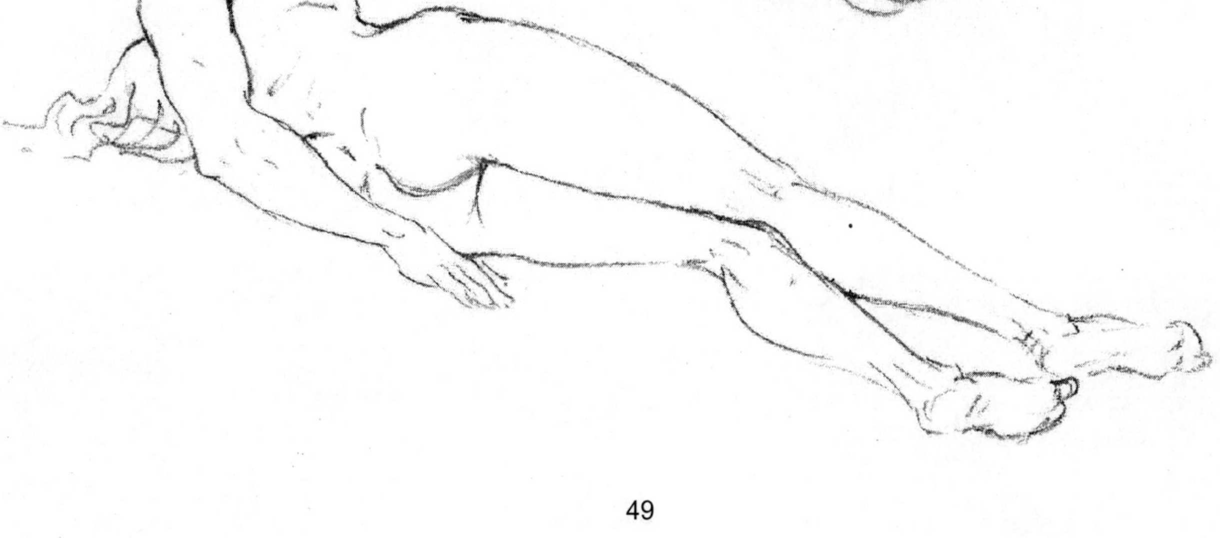

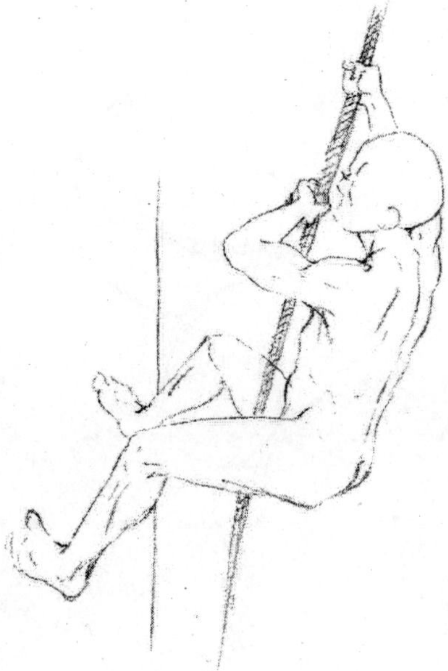

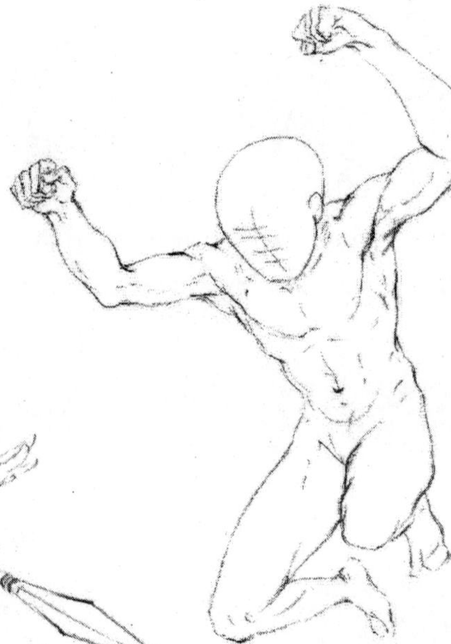

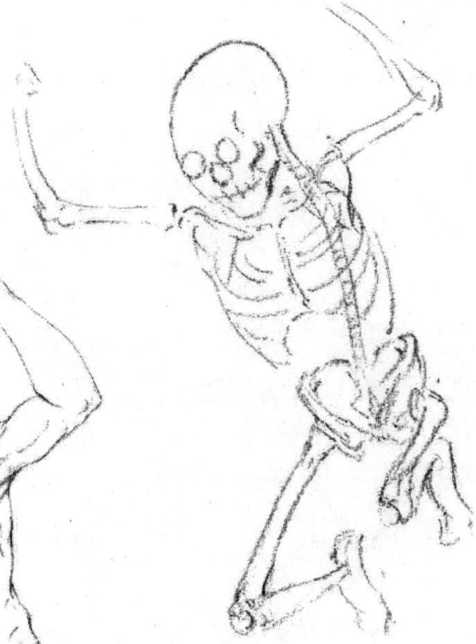

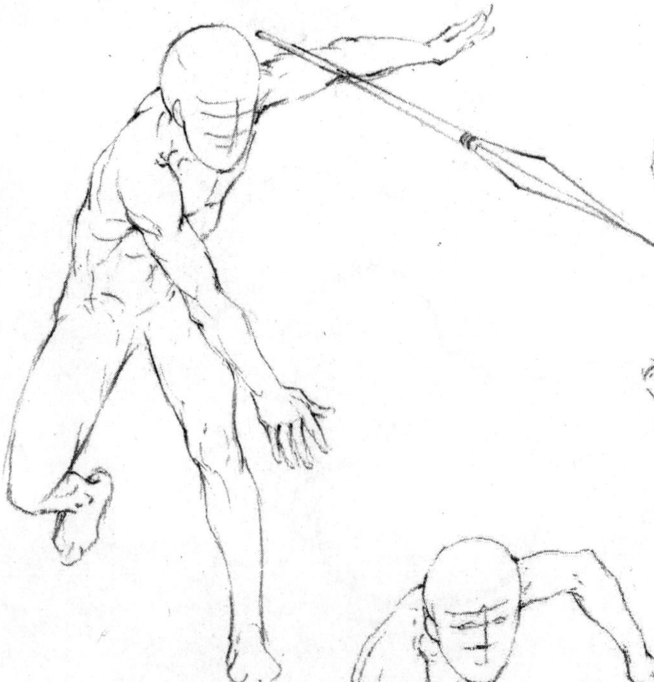

Once you have decided upon what you want to draw, make sure that it should convert into a beautiful figure drawing.

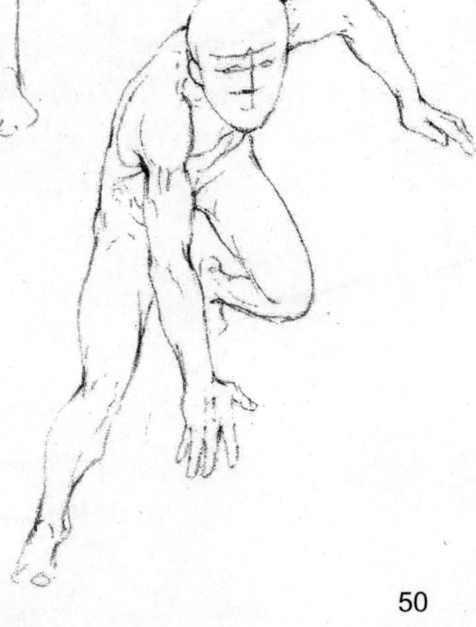

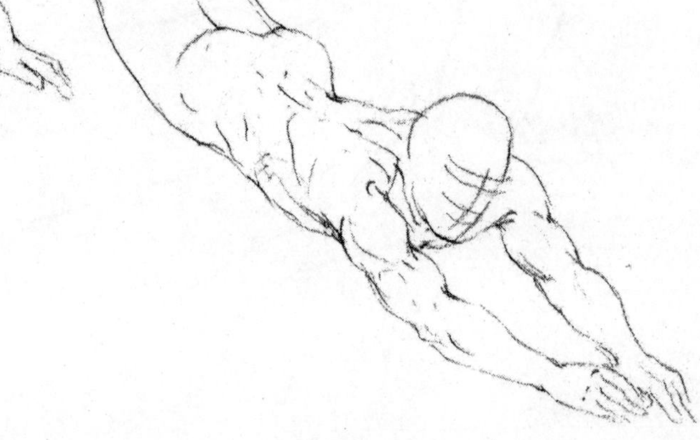

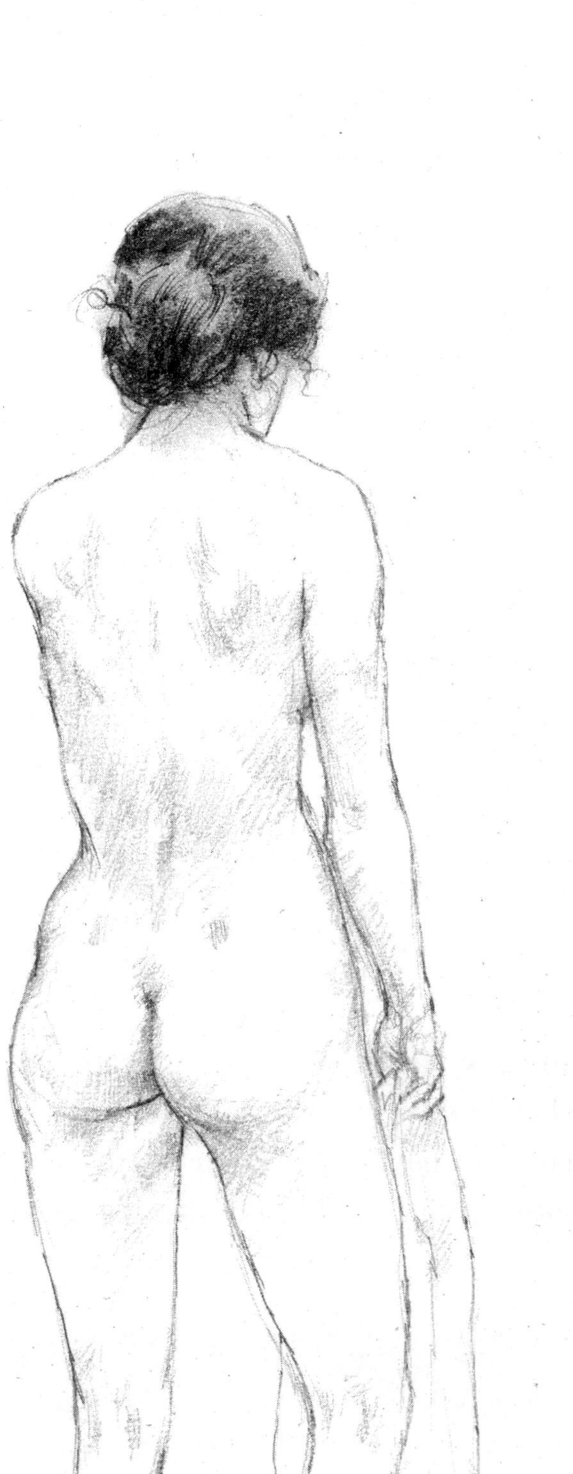

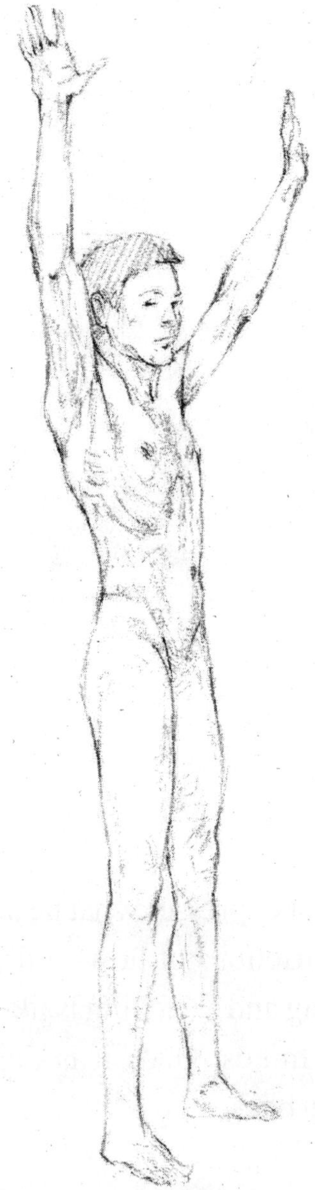

You must establish the scale of your composition by indicating its limits. Take your measurements from the point of the bony structure, rather than from the fleshy edges.

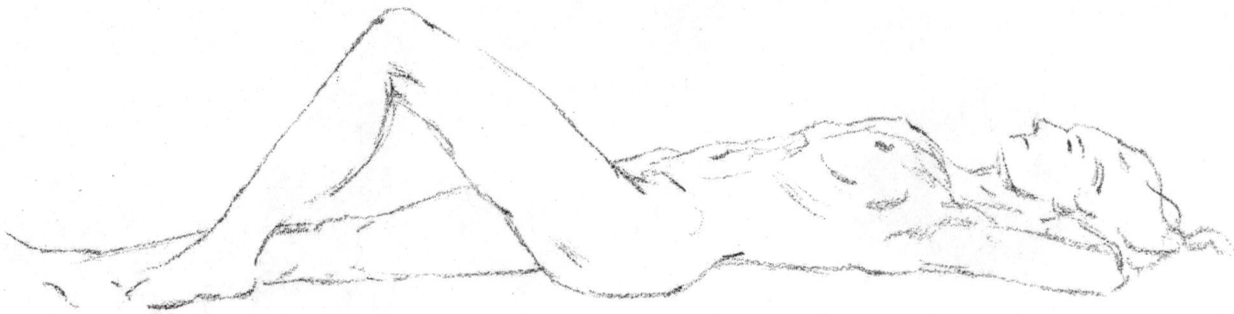

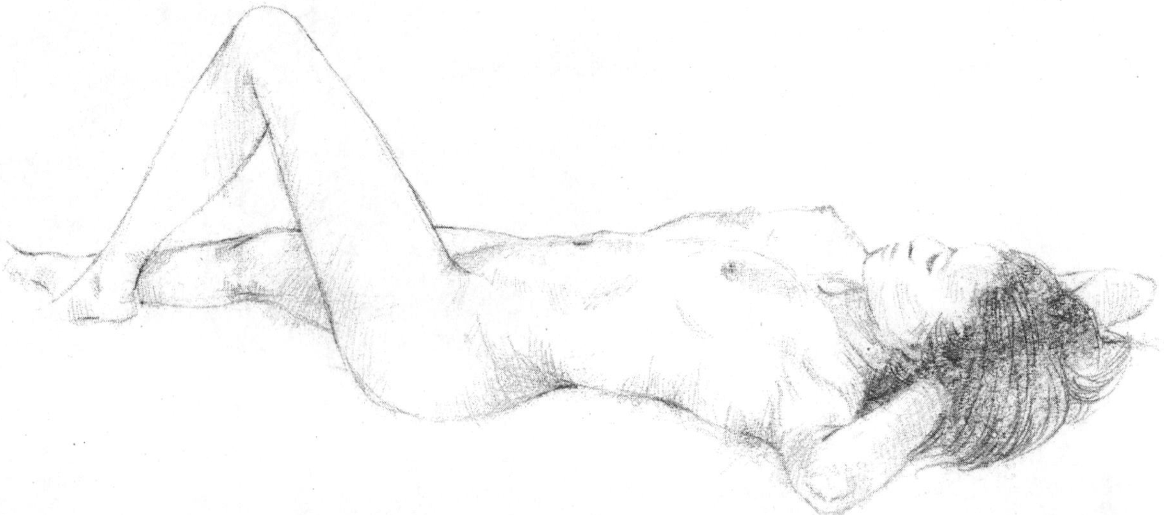

An artist expresses what he sees in terms of lines and forms. We only have to put aside the restrictions of how to draw and of what quality and we can be artists ourselves. Drawing and sketching is like living, and we only have to put the right type of thoughts in our minds. Once it is done and we start getting positive results, we will not be looking back.

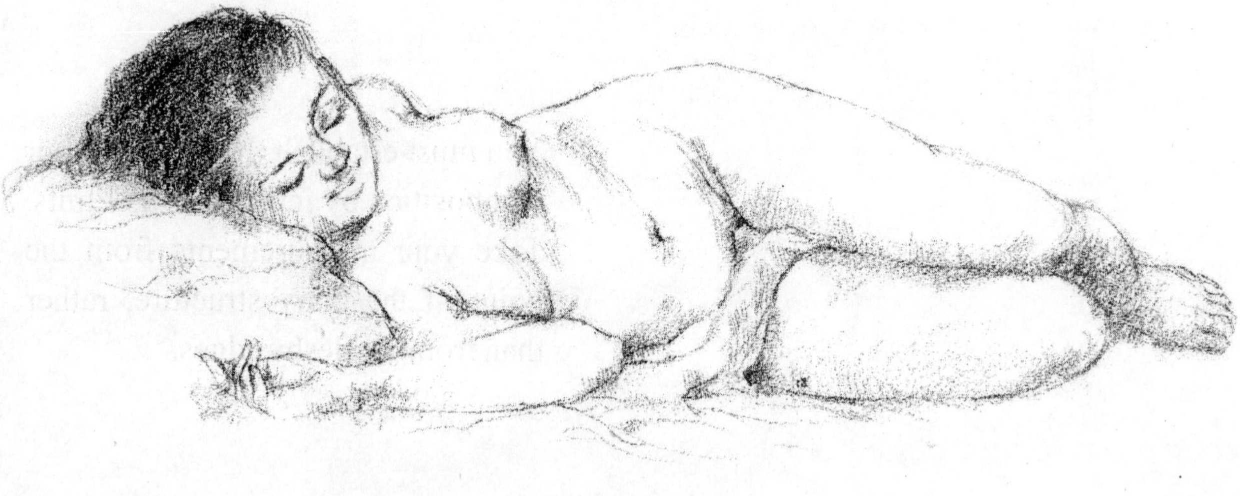

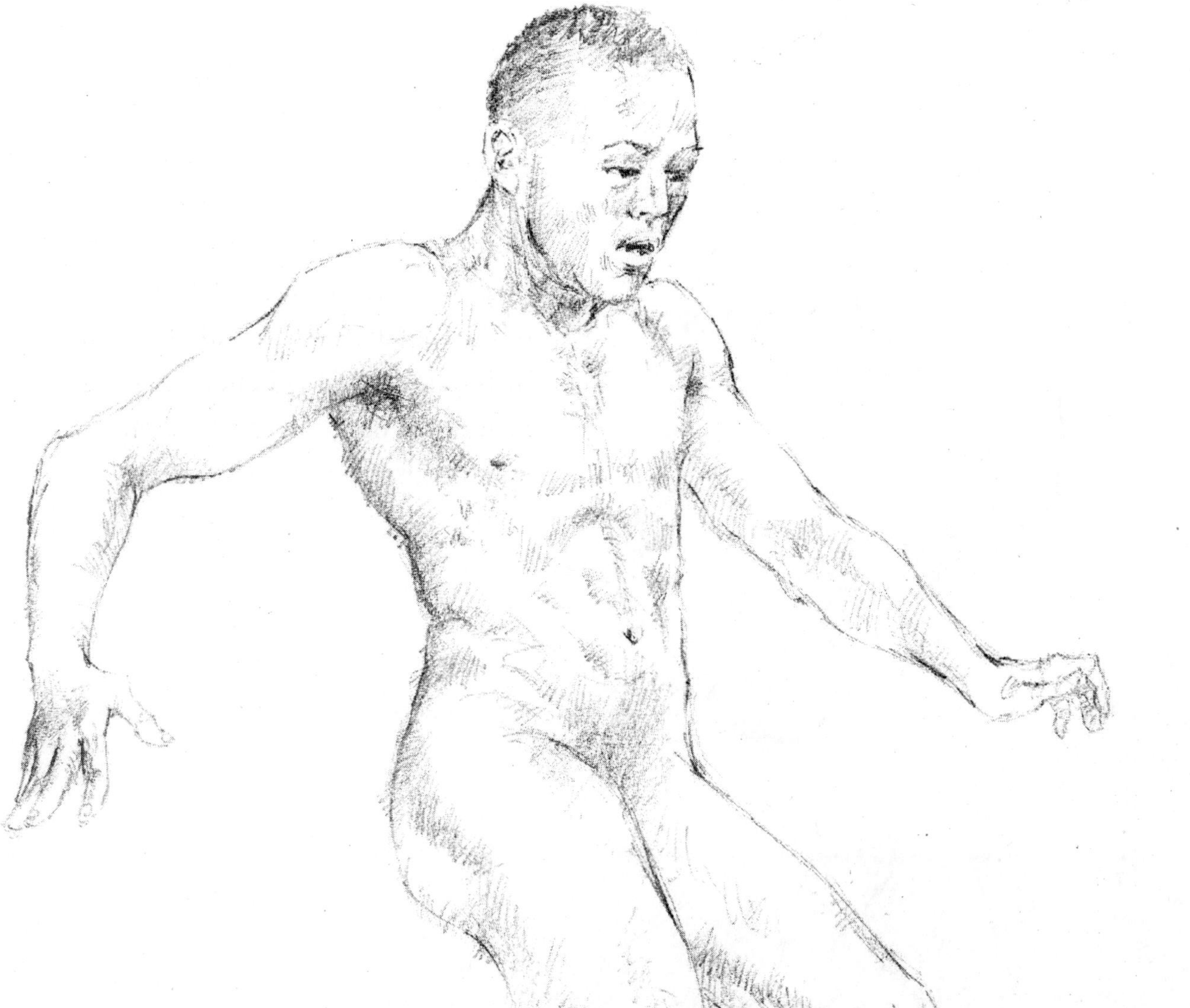

How to Draw Feet

This picture shows the movement of a foot. The toes and the volume of the foot are shown with the help of block drawing. Pencil shading brings out the drawing's character and the dimension step by step.

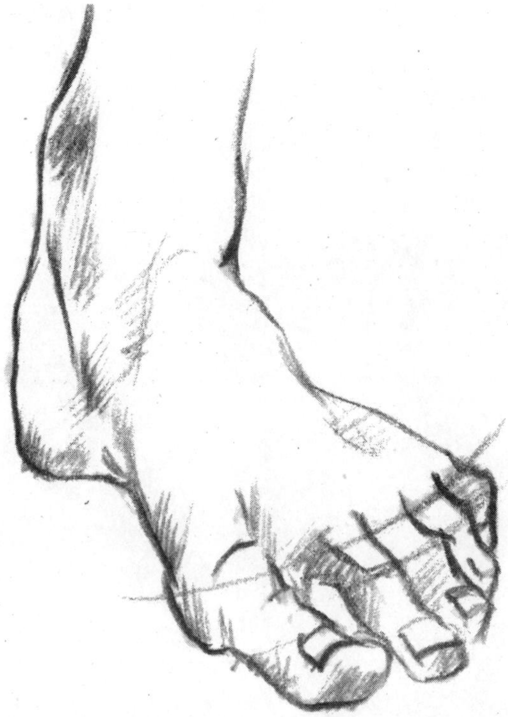

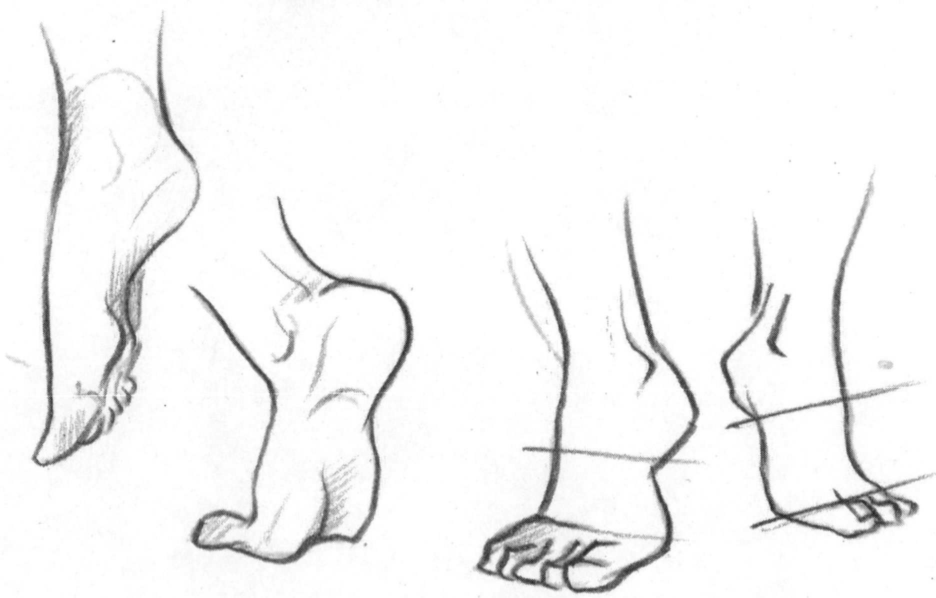

As shown in the picture above, with the help of block drawing, in these figures, we show the front foot and the side foot. Line drawing and pencil shade have been used to create thickness and volume. We can do figure drawing in a similar manner.

How to Finish

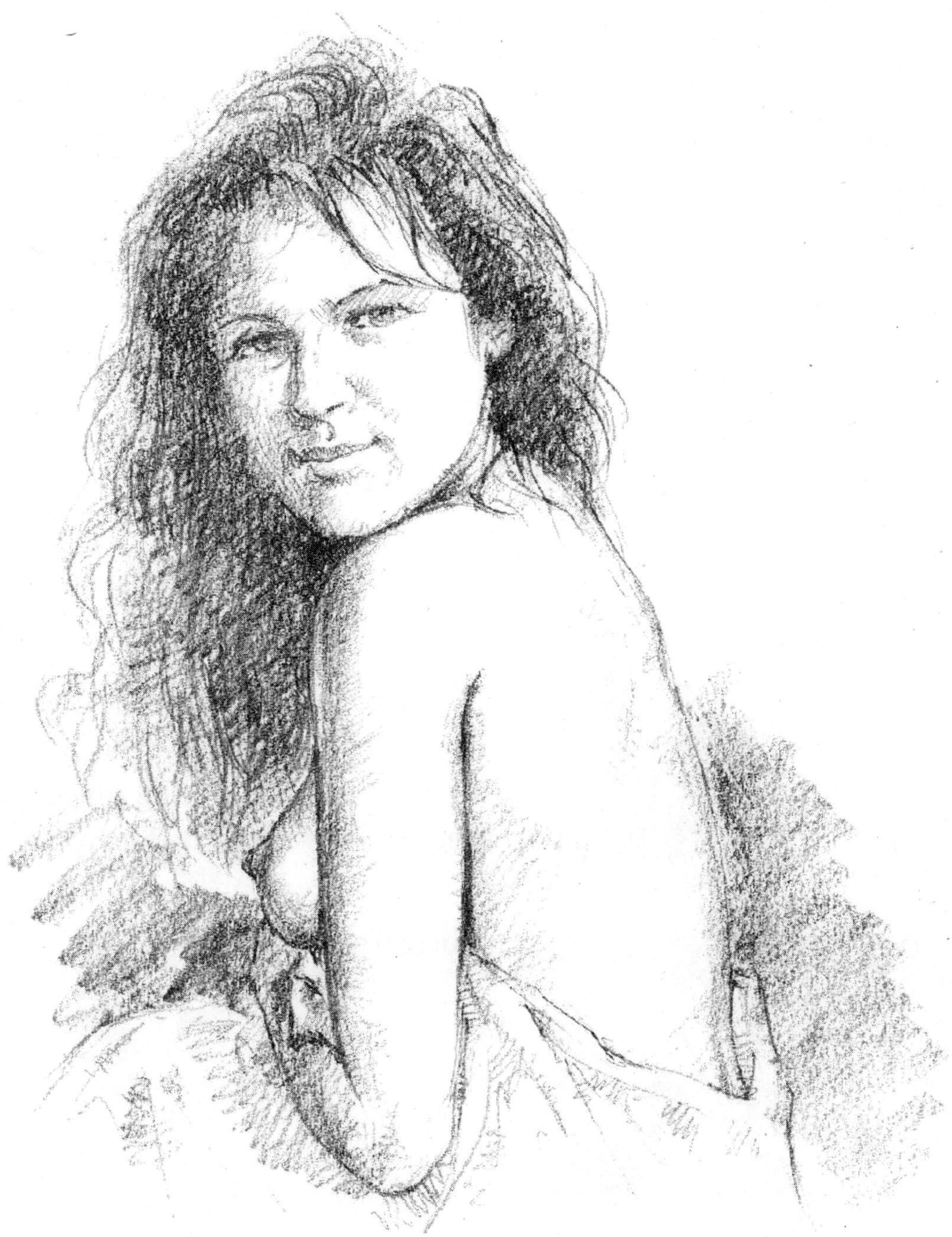

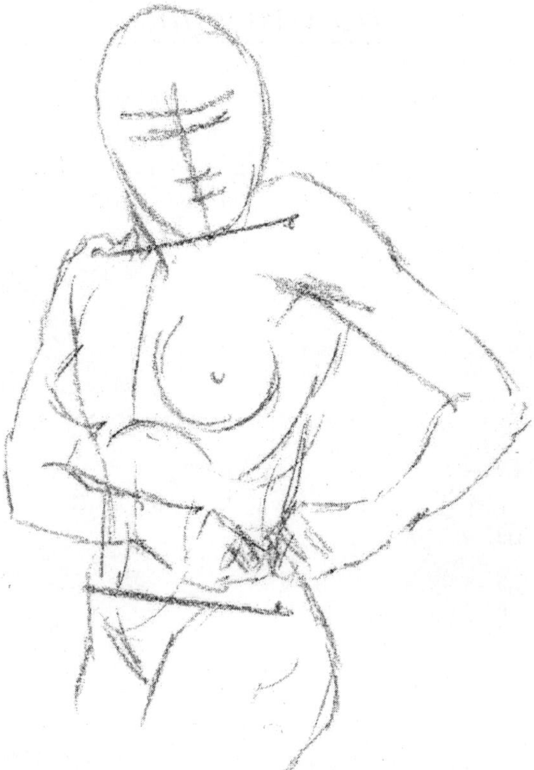

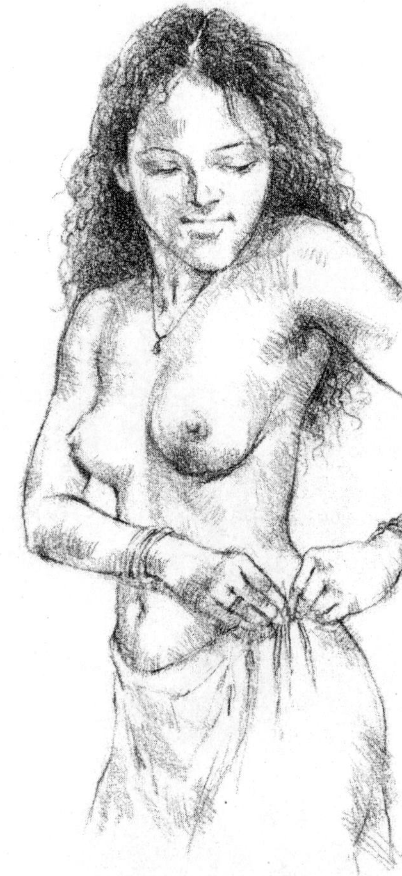

If you have selected a photograph to draw, remember that you will have to create the perspective by diffusing things which are placed further and away from you.

Study the effect of light by placing the lamp at different angles.

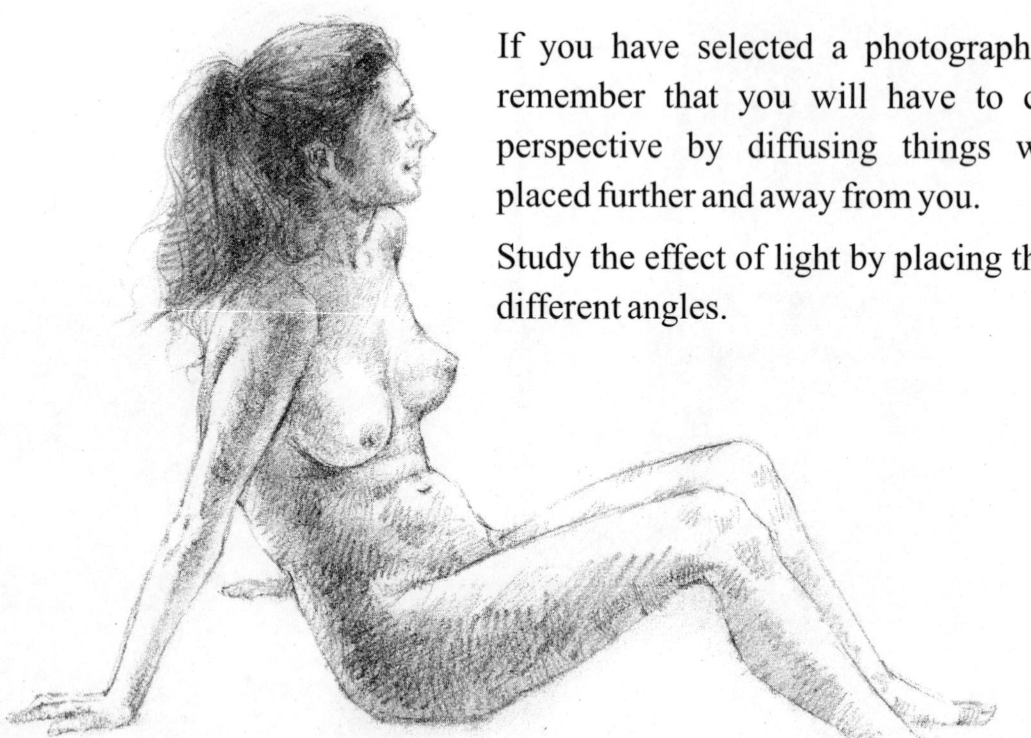

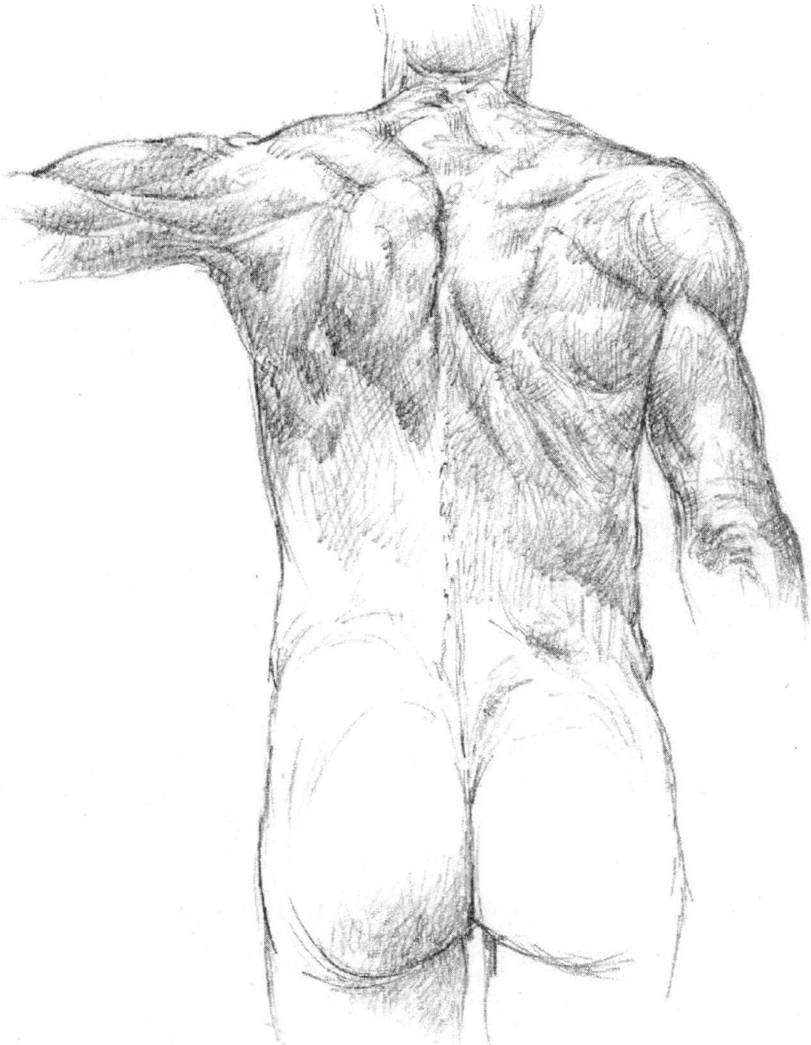

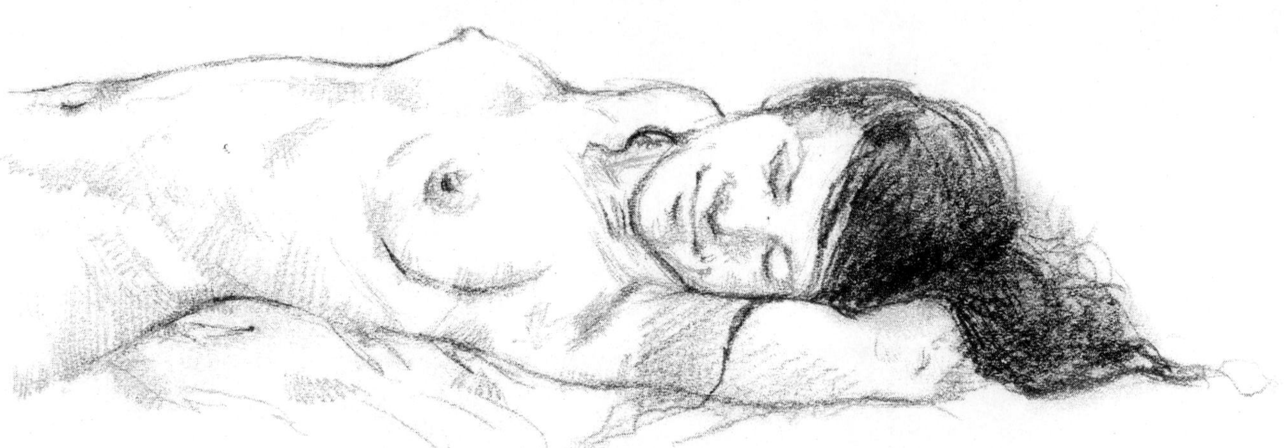

A female body consists of a series of cylindrical forms. The torso, arms, legs and even the fingers and toes belong to different such shapes. The head is oval shaped, eyes are like balls set in hollow sockets, and the nose is projected in a cone like formation.

Make soft, structural lines to capture the pose of your subject.

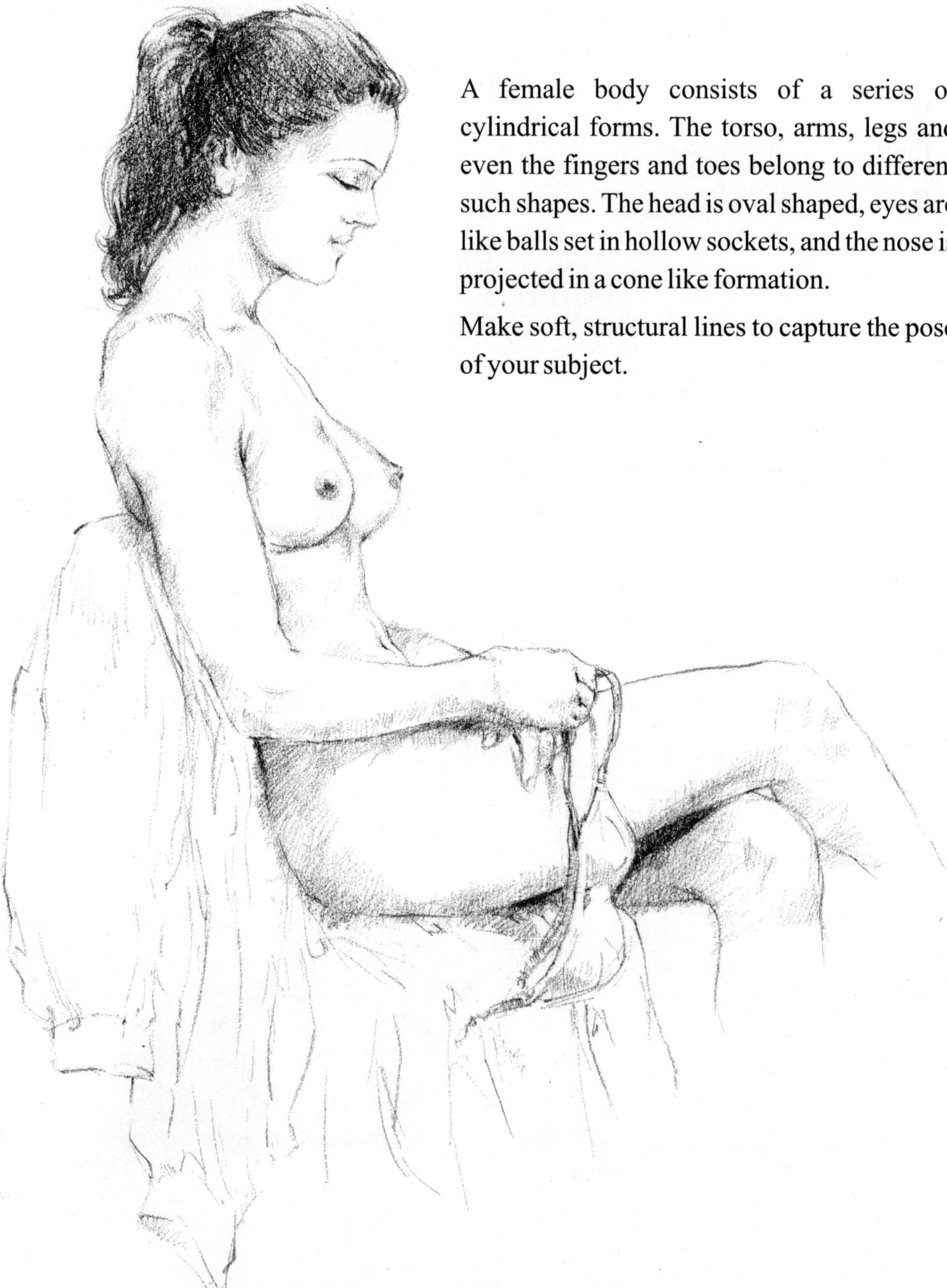

Draw fast, as only speed can catch a movement. Avoid unnecessary details in the finished drawing because you will lose spontaneity in your sketch if you do it.

Basically there are three shapes in nature - the sphere, cube and the cone. If we extend these then we will have cylindrical and oblong shapes.

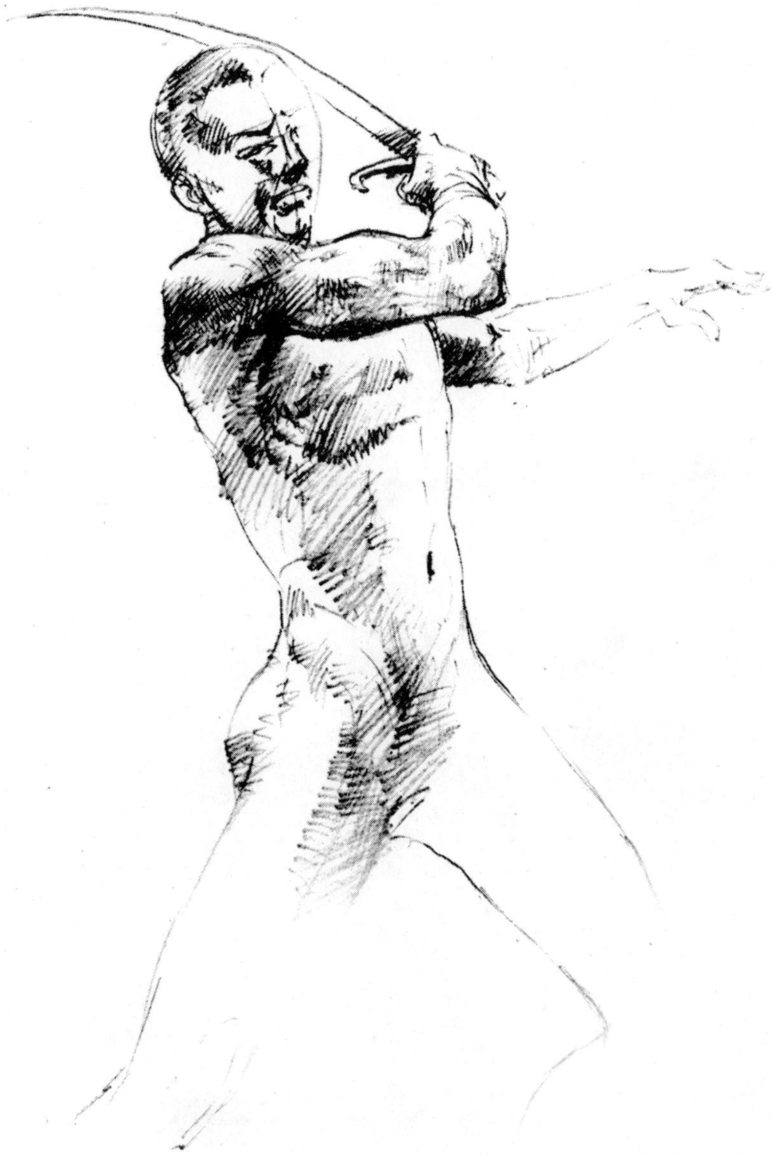

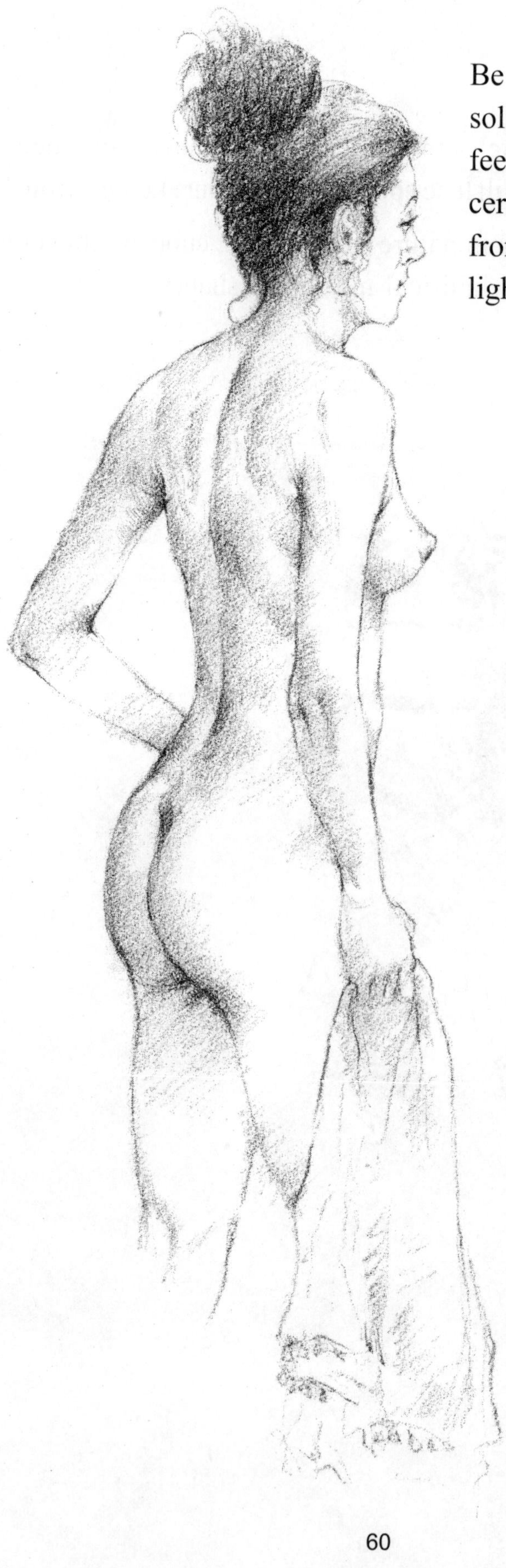

Be conscious of the body's weight and solidity when you are drawing. Try to feel the volume and softness of a certain body part. Due to reflections from nearby forms, shadows have light in them. They are not solids.

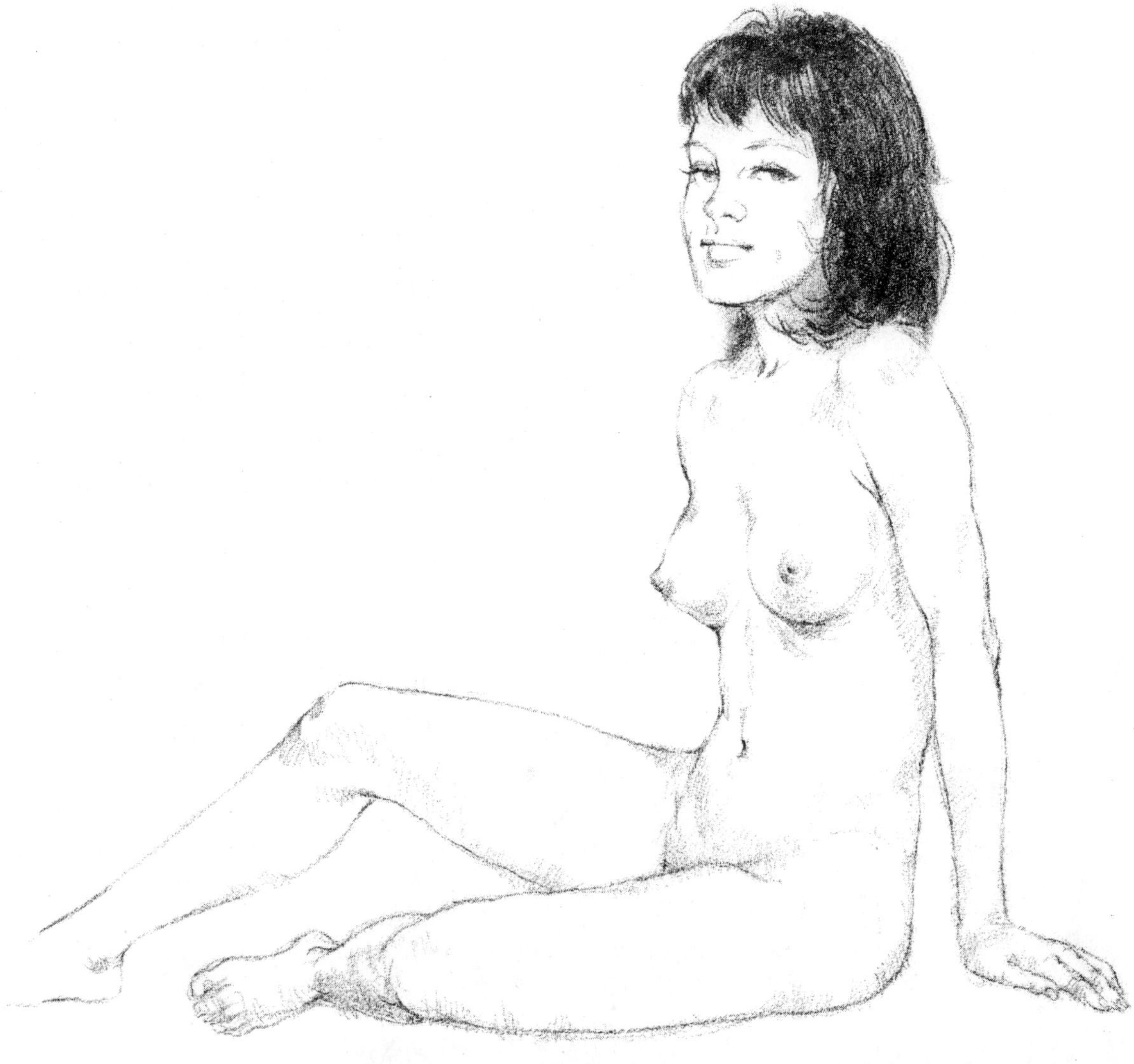

A fine line drawing contains the whole summary of whatever you want to express, so keep things simple but accurate. You should be able to recognise the basic and structural forms in a certain pose. The larger and smaller areas may differ in size but the volume and form will always be there.

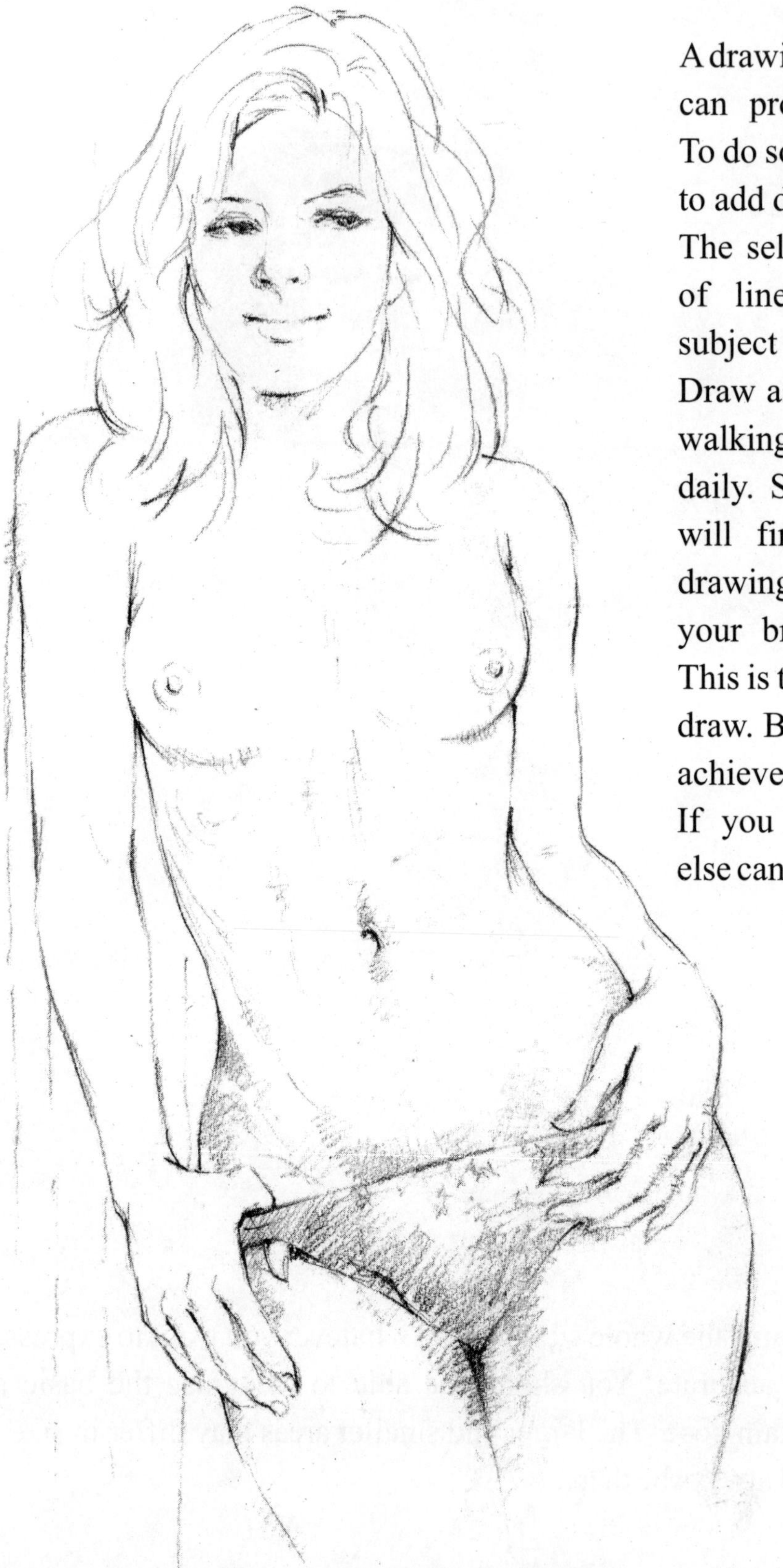

A drawing is a dream which you can produce in your sketch. To do so, you must know where to add details and when to stop. The selection of various types of lines for describing the subject is also very important. Draw as much as you can, like walking, talking and smiling daily. Someday, suddenly you will find that your hand is drawing automatically without your brain thinking about it. This is the real and ideal state to draw. But it takes some time to achieve. Love your drawings. If you don't like it, nobody else can.

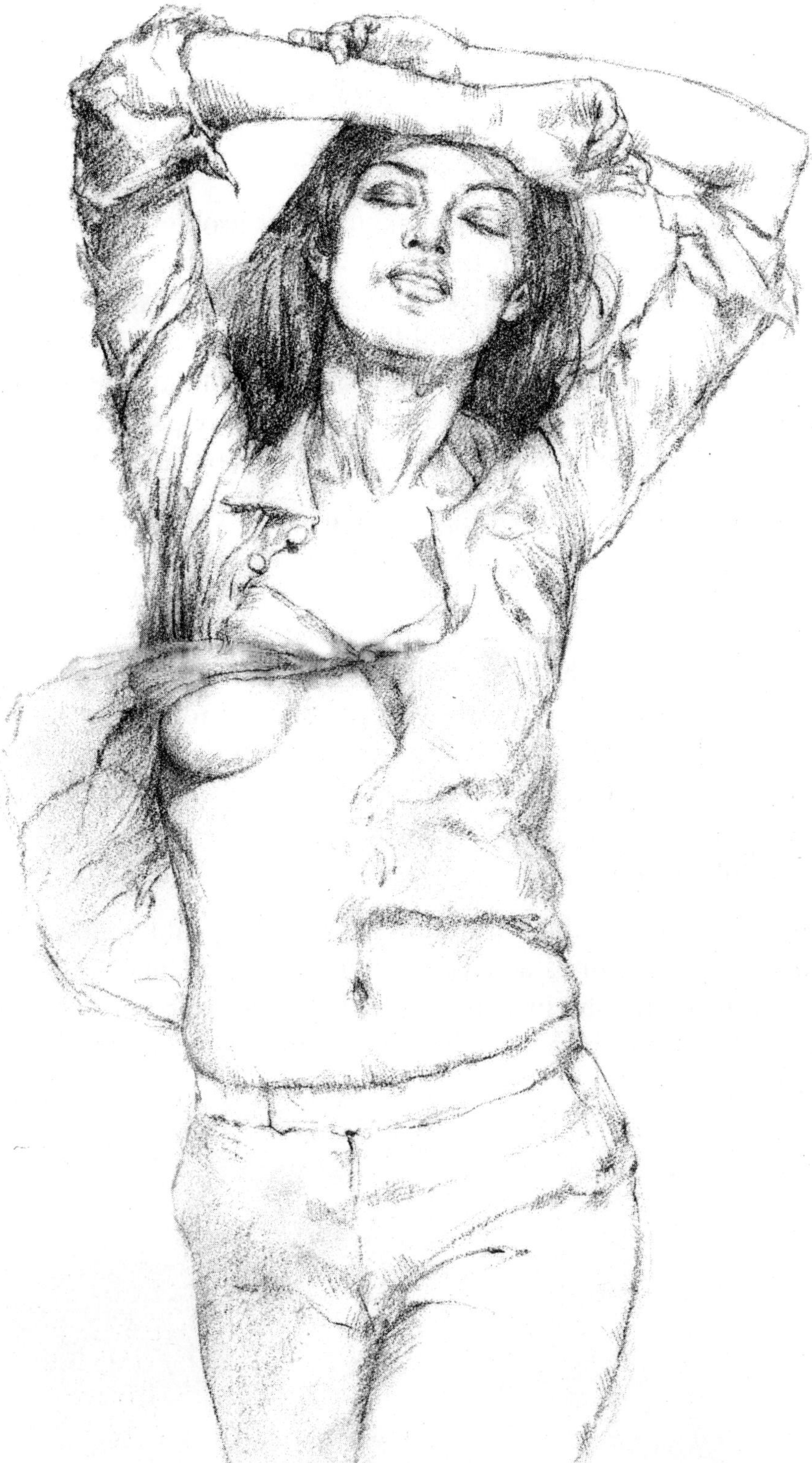

Always draw in a natural way which is most suitable for you. Here natural way means what is natural to you, which suits you well. If you want to add lot of detail, do it. If you like to work in a few defining lines, it is good. Keep things simple, simplicity is the ultimate attainment of art and beginning of nature and when drawing becomes natural to you, than with time you will become your own teacher. So take things as they come in your life and keep drawing every thing you like.

Whoever can hold a pencil can draw or sketch. The problem arises only when you start comparing your drawing with those of others and add some definition to it. We our selves are the main obstacles in our progress as an artist and the cause lies with false conceptions. How about your childhood when things were not so tough for you? When drawing a complex landscape consisting of mountains, trees, rivers and of course, a small hut was so easy. It was so, because then we were used to expressing things in a very simple way. What we have lost today is the great confidence which we had.

As you see, when you draw something, no matter how clumsy, poor or dirty it is, it still is a drawing and with every passing day it will certainly improve. "Oh.. It is all dreams", you will say. Well do me a favour, draw a very simple thing for me. A tea pot will do. Put it on the table and draw it as you see it. Do not think about good or bad. Just repeat for five consecutive days. Put the date on it everyday and add some notes only if you think you saw or found something new in it. On the third or fourth day you will suddenly be able to see some shades, lights and dimensions. Go on, now, if you think I am trying to fool you. I assure you, once, only once if you do it, you will be an artist because once you get results with a small unimportant and simple object, you will go for more complex things. This is human nature.

Every artist starts with the three triangles representing mountains, a circle as sun and two curved, unbalanced lines as river. When some day this same person draws your portrait, you seem to transfer on paper with life sparking in your eyes. This Mr. X can be you, if you think it is worth trying. The positive thoughts and daily diddling with pencil will do the rest.

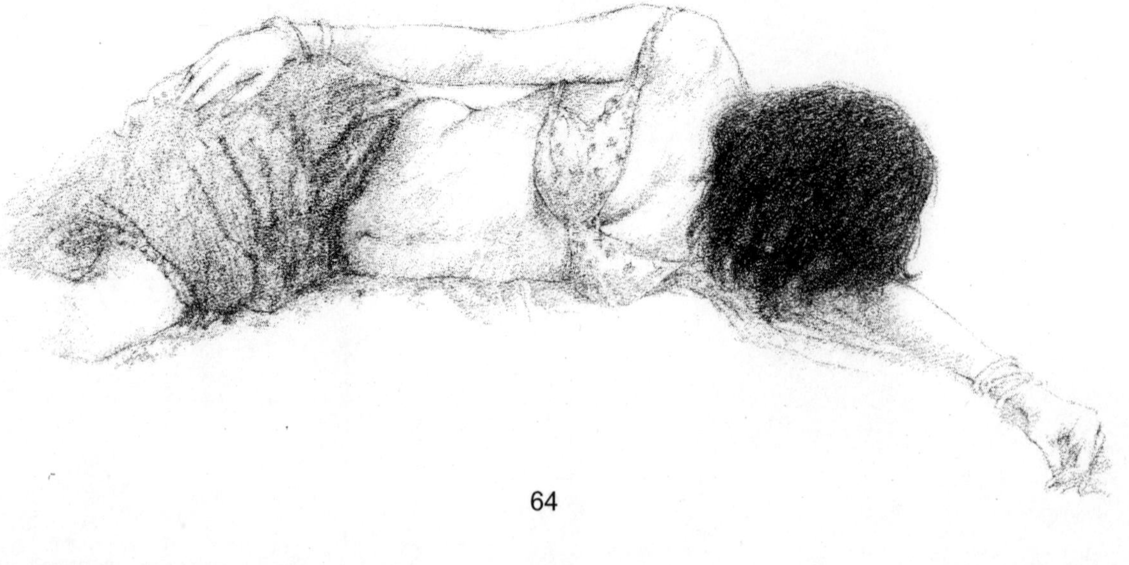